To Kara,

So many great times in D.C. was amazing and your Dad.

You have an obligation now to use your brains and ambition to perhaps return to D.C. and make the changes this country needs. My best to you always. It was an honor to had been your teacher

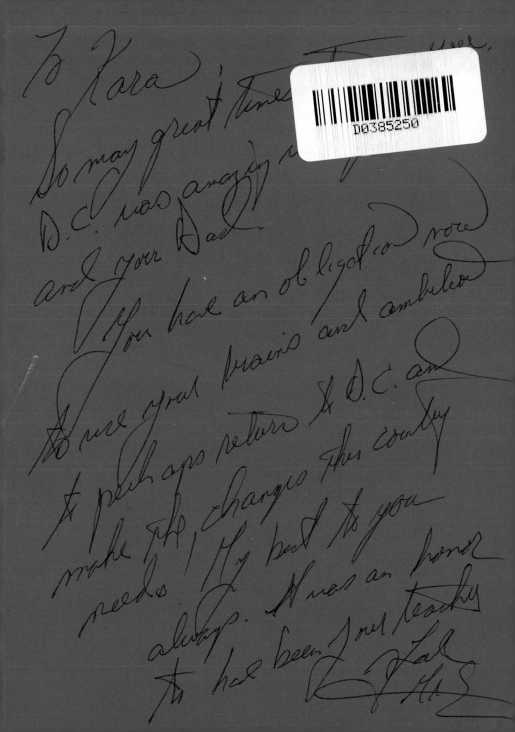

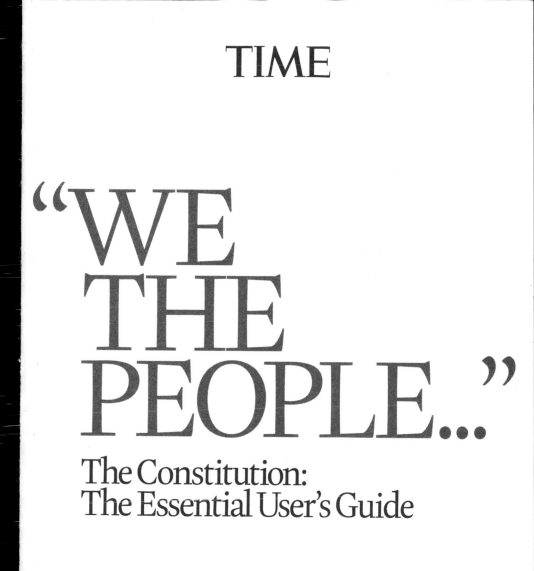

TIME

"WE THE PEOPLE..."

The Constitution:
The Essential User's Guide

TIME

MANAGING EDITOR Richard Stengel
DESIGN DIRECTOR D.W. Pine
DIRECTOR OF PHOTOGRAPHY Kira Pollack

EDITOR / ANNOTATOR Richard Lacayo
DESIGNER Arthur Hochstein
PHOTO EDITOR Richard Boeth
RESEARCHER Kathleen Adams
COPY EDITOR Erik Rhey
EDITORIAL PRODUCTION David Sloan

TIME HOME ENTERTAINMENT

PUBLISHER Richard Fraiman
VICE PRESIDENT, BUSINESS DEVELOPMENT AND STRATEGY Steven Sandonato
EXECUTIVE DIRECTOR, MARKETING SERVICES Carol Pittard
EXECUTIVE DIRECTOR, RETAIL AND SPECIAL SALES Tom Mifsud
EXECUTIVE PUBLISHING DIRECTOR Joy Butts
DIRECTOR, BOOKAZINE DEVELOPMENT AND MARKETING Laura Adam
FINANCE DIRECTOR Glenn Buonocore
ASSISTANT GENERAL COUNSEL Helen Wan
ASSISTANT DIRECTOR, SPECIAL SALES Ilene Schreider
BOOK PRODUCTION MANAGER Suzanne Janso
DESIGN AND PREPRESS MANAGER Anne-Michelle Gallero
BRAND MANAGER Michela Wilde

EDITORIAL DIRECTOR Stephen Koepp

SPECIAL THANKS TO: Christine Austin, Jeremy Biloon, Jim Childs, Susan Chodakiewicz, Rose Cirrincione, Lauren Hall Clark, Jacqueline Fitzgerald, Hillary Hirsch, Christine Font, Jenna Goldberg, Amy Mangus, Robert Marasco, Kimberly Marshall, Amy Migliaccio, Nina Mistry, Dave Rozzelle, Adriana Tierno, Alex Voznesenskiy, Vanessa Wu, Isata Yansaneh, Time Imaging

A STATUE OF JOHN BARRY,
"FATHER OF THE U.S. NAVY,"
GESTURES SKYWARD OUTSIDE
INDEPENDENCE HALL,
BIRTHPLACE OF
THE CONSTITUTION

THE HAND OF A SCULPTED
FIGURE IN THE SIGNERS'
HALL OF THE NATIONAL
CONSTITUTION CENTER
IN PHILADELPHIA

CONTENTS

The Annotated U.S. Constitution

To Preserve And Protect...

By Sandra Day O'Connor

S OME PEOPLE QUESTION WHETHER THE U.S. CONSTITUTION lives up to the needs of modern citizens. I think a fairer question is whether modern citizens—We, the People—are living up to the needs of our Constitution. Our government relies on good citizens. To be a good citizen, you need to know how our government works. And to do that, you need to know the Constitution.

We, the People, have room to improve. One poll from a few years ago tells us that less than half of Americans can name the three branches of government—yet three-quarters can name each of the Three Stooges. These days not many Americans are even inspired to take a closer look. In another poll 57% of Americans admit to having little to no confidence in Congress.

Even as trust in government and other institutions plummets, the good news is that many Americans continue to look to the Constitution (not Moe, Larry, and Curly) for answers. Doing so brings us back to our roots, to the enduring principles and ideals that animated our nation's founding. Now, as we celebrate the 225th anniversary of the Constitution, it is time to rediscover and deepen our understanding of those principles.

Sandra Day O'Connor is a retired associate justice of the U.S. Supreme Court (1981–2006) and founder of iCivics.org.

As we reflect on the triumph of the Constitutional Convention, we recognize that today—much like in the summer of 1787—reasonable minds can disagree on some major principles. Indeed, sometimes it seems that the Constitution is wielded more often as a sword than as a solution in increasingly partisan debates over issues. But it is a testament to the enduring nature of our founding document that it inspires the passion of people in the Tea Party as well as in Occupy Wall Street. As we strive to sustain our tradition of freedom and confront the challenges of our day, all of us should recommit ourselves to the Constitution and to the active citizenship that makes our Constitution and government work.

What makes the Constitution worthy of our commitment? First and foremost, the answer is our freedom. It is, quite simply, the most powerful vision of human freedom ever expressed. It's also the world's shortest and oldest national constitution, neither so rigid as to be stifling, nor so malleable as to be devoid of meaning.

Our Constitution has been an inspiration that changed the trajectory of world history for the perpetual benefit of mankind. In 1787, no country in the world had ever allowed its citizens to select their own form of government, much less to select a democratic government. What was revolutionary when it was written, and what continues to inspire the world today, is that the Constitution put governance in the hands of the people. Today, 225 years later, more than half the nations on earth are democratic.

Visit the National Constitution Center in Philadelphia—just steps away from Independence Hall, where the Constitution was drafted—and watch the reactions of visitors, especially children, to the stirring

> "WE SHOULD BE PARTICULARLY CONCERNED THAT THE DECLINE IN CIVIC EDUCATION IS UNDERMINING AMERICANS' UNDERSTANDING OF AND FAITH IN OUR COURTS AND THE JUDICIAL PROCESS."
> —JUSTICE O'CONNOR

images of immigrants becoming American citizens in naturalization ceremonies. It could hardly be more clear how much our newest citizens value that which many Americans now take for granted: our freedom, our American ideals, our Constitution.

It is exactly our tendency to take our freedoms and our Constitution for granted that spurs the greatest challenge facing our democracy today: a near-failure of civic education. Virtually all the Founding Fathers recognized that democracy depends on a well-informed public. James Madison, one of the principal architects of the Constitution, put it this way: "A popular Government, without popular information, or the means of acquiring it, is but a Prologue to a Farce or a Tragedy; or, perhaps both. ...A people who mean to be their own Governors, must arm themselves with the power which knowledge gives."

Today, 40 state constitutions tout the importance of civic knowledge, and 13—some predating our national constitution—cite civic education as the primary purpose of schools. It is hard to disagree that we are failing in this civic mission of schools when more than two-thirds of American students perform below proficiency in the U.S. Department of Education's national civics assessment, and less than 20% of twelfth graders can explain how citizen participation benefits democracy.

We should be particularly concerned that the decline in civic education is undermining Americans' understanding of and faith in our courts and the judicial process. In a 2006 survey commissioned by the Annenberg Public Policy Center at the University of Pennsylvania, four in ten Americans believe that the president may constitutionally ignore a Supreme Court ruling. We are increasingly seeing citizens attacking judges for their rulings. We hear calls for an elected judiciary and for the impeachment or removal of judges. But when American citizens perceive judges as politicians in robes, rather than unbiased arbiters of the law, we risk losing the independence of our judiciary, which is a cornerstone of our Constitution and of our freedom.

Nevertheless, there are seeds of solutions. Even as the civics and social studies classes that many readers of this book remember have become anachronisms along with chalkboards and instructional filmstrips, new media solutions for informing and engaging students are emerging. In 2009 I founded iCivics (www.icivics.org), a free, online civics curriculum for middle school and high school students that uses online role-playing games, videos, social networking, and other activities to engage students on a pathway to lifelong civic participation. And for those of you who are my age and shuddering at the idea of teaching constitutional principles on Facebook, remember that the principle "If you can't beat 'em, join 'em," was one of the practical rules of compromise used in crafting and ratifying the Constitution itself.

There is a direct correlation between civic knowledge and what the political philosopher William A. Galston has called "political participation, expression of democratic values including toleration, stable political attitudes, and adoption of enlightened self-interest." Teachers and parents—who are the first and best civics teachers, because they teach by example—should make it clear to children: Civics isn't just important, it is empowering. Beyond the classroom, each of us has the opportunity to engage in the American experiment of democracy. We can start with ourselves and our families. We can vote, we can write to our representatives, we can volunteer in our community. We can push for stronger civic education in our schools. We can read books—like this one—to develop and deepen our own understanding of the Constitution. When the president takes the oath of office, he swears to "preserve, protect, and defend the Constitution of the United States."

We, the People, can and must do the same.

We the People

of the U[nited States, in Order to form a more perfect Union, establish Justice,]
insure domestic Tranquility, provide for the common defence, pr[omote the general Welfare,]
and our Posterity, do ordain and establish this Constitution for th[e United States of America.]

Article. I

Section. 1. All legislative Powers herein granted shall be vested [in a Congress of the United States, which shall consist of a Senate and House]
of Representatives.

Section. 2. The House of Representatives shall be composed of M[embers chosen every second Year by the People of the several States, and the Electors]
in each State shall have the Qualifications requisite for Electors of the most nu[merous Branch of the State Legislature.]

No Person shall be a Representative who shall not have attain[ed to the Age of twenty five Years, and been seven Years a Citizen of the United States,]
and who shall not, when elected, be an Inhabitant of that State in which he [shall be chosen.]

Representatives and direct Taxes shall be apportioned among the se[veral States which may be included within this Union, according to their respective]
Numbers, which shall be determined by adding to the whole Number of fre[e Persons, including those bound to Service for a Term of Years, and excluding Indians]
not taxed, three fifths of all other Persons. The actual Enumeration sha[ll be made within three Years after the first Meeting of the Congress of the United States,]
and within every subsequent Term of ten Years, in such Manner as they [shall by Law direct. The Number of Representatives shall not exceed one for every]
thirty Thousand, but each State shall have at Least one Representative; [and until such enumeration shall be made, the State of New Hampshire shall be]
entitled to chuse three, Massachusetts eight, Rhode Island and Provide[nce Plantations one, Connecticut five, New-York six, New Jersey four, Pennsylvania]
eight, Delaware one, Maryland six, Virginia ten, North Carolina five, [South Carolina five, and Georgia three.]

When vacancies happen in the Representation from any State, [the Executive Authority thereof shall issue Writs of Election to fill such Vacancies.]

The House of Representatives shall chuse their Speaker and othe[r Officers; and shall have the sole Power of Impeachment.]

Section. 3. The Senate of the United States shall be composed of two [Senators from each State, chosen by the Legislature thereof, for six Years; and each]
Senator shall have one Vote.

Immediately after they shall be assembled in Consequence of the [first Election, they shall be divided as equally as may be into three Classes. The Seats]
of the Senators of the first Class shall be vacated at the Expiration of the se[cond Year, of the second Class at the Expiration of the fourth Year, and of the third]
Class at the Expiration of the sixth Year, so that one third may be chosen ev[ery second Year; and if Vacancies happen by Resignation, or otherwise, during the]
Recess of the Legislature of any State, the Executive thereof may make tempor[ary Appointments until the next Meeting of the Legislature, which shall then fill]
such Vacancies.

No Person shall be a Senator who shall not have attained to the [Age of thirty Years, and been nine Years a Citizen of the United States, and who shall]
not, when elected, be an Inhabitant of that State for which he shall be chose[n.]

The Vice President of the United States shall be President of the Se[nate, but shall have no Vote, unless they be equally divided.]

The Senate shall chuse their other Officers, and also a President, pro [tempore, in the Absence of the Vice President, or when he shall exercise the Office of]
President of the United States.

The Senate shall have the sole Power to try all Impeachments. W[hen sitting for that Purpose, they shall be on Oath or Affirmation.]

One Document, Under Siege

By Richard Stengel

ERE ARE A FEW THINGS THE FRAMERS DID NOT KNOW about: World War II. DNA. Sexting. Airplanes. The atom. Television. Medicare. Collateralized debt obligations. The germ theory of disease. Miniskirts. The internal combustion engine. Computers. Antibiotics. Lady Gaga.

People on the right and left constantly ask what the framers would say about some event that is happening in our own time. What would the framers say about whether the drones authorized by President Obama and being used over Pakistan constitute a violation of Article I, Section 8, which gives Congress the power to declare war? Well, since George Washington didn't even dream that man could fly, much less use a global-positioning satellite to aim a missile, it's hard to say what he would think. What would the framers say about whether a tax on people who did not buy health insurance is an abuse of Congress's authority under the commerce clause? Well, since James Madison did not know what health insurance was and doctors back then still used leeches, it's difficult to know what he would say. And what would any of the framers who were slave owners have thought of a half-white, half-black

Richard Stengel is managing editor of TIME Magazine and former president and CEO of the National Constitution Center in Philadelphia

American president born in Hawaii, a state that did not exist in 1787? Again, hard to say.

The framers were not gods and were not infallible. Yes, they gave us and the world a blueprint for republican government and for the protection of democratic freedoms—freedom of speech, assembly, religion—but they also gave us the idea that a black person who was a slave was three-fifths of a human being, that women were not allowed to vote, and that South Dakota should have the same number of Senators as California, which is kind of crazy. And I'm not even going to mention the electoral college. They did not give us income taxes. Or Prohibition. Those came later.

But whether or not the framers knew about drones or computers or rap music doesn't really matter. The Constitution represents fundamental principles of democratic government and embodies the values of a free society. Yes, it is the supreme law of the land, but it is not a code of laws or regulations, or even applications of those legal principles. It doesn't tell you whether crossing against a red light is a felony, but it does tell you that restricting free speech is inimical to a free society. So when it comes to the vexing issues of our time, we need to look at the values and principles represented by the Constitution, not whether Alexander Hamilton ever used the internet. The examples change and will always change; the underlying principles do not.

Still, those principles evolve and how they are adapted to contemporary situations is not always clear. The nature of those principles and the specific ways they are to be applied are still being debated and, one hopes, always will be. Americans have argued about the Constitution since the day it was signed, but seldom have so many disagreed so fiercely about so much. Would it be unconstitutional to default on our debt? Is it a violation of the First Amendment to require church-affiliated institutions to have health plans that cover birth control for their employees? Should we have a balanced-budget amendment? Is it constitutional to ask illegal immigrants to carry documents? The first decade of the 21st century, beginning with the disputed election of 2000, has been a long national civics class about what the Constitution means—and how much it still matters. For eight years under George W. Bush, the nation

EACH GENERATION HAS FACED ISSUES THAT TRIGGERED DEBATE OVER THE
MEANING OF THE CONSTITUTION, INCLUDING (CLOCKWISE FROM TOP LEFT)
THE CIVIL RIGHTS MOVEMENT, THE KOREAN WAR, THE SHOOTING OF REP.
GABRIELLE GIFFORDS, AND THE WATERGATE SCANDAL

wrestled with the balance between privacy and security (an issue the framers contended with) while the left portrayed the country as moving toward tyranny. Under President Obama, we have weighed issues of individual freedom vs. government control while the right portrayed the country as moving toward a socialist welfare state.

A new focus on the Constitution is at the center of our political stage with the rise of the Tea Party and its almost fanatical focus on the founding document. To open its first session in 2011, the new Republican Congress organized a reading on the House floor of all 7,200 words of the Constitution and its amendments. The Republican candidates for president all depict themselves as fierce defenders and trusted interpreters of the Constitution. As a counterpoint to the rise of constitutional originalists (those who believe the document should be interpreted only as the drafters understood it), liberal legal scholars analyze the text just as closely to find the elasticity they believe the framers intended. Everywhere there seems to be debate about the scope and meaning and message of the Constitution. This is a healthy thing. Even the framers would agree on that.

So are we in a constitutional crisis? In a word, no. The Constitution was born in crisis. It was written in secret and in violation of the existing one, the very weak Articles of Confederation, which failed to create an effective central government. It was born at a time when no one knew whether America would survive. The Constitution has never not been under threat. Benjamin Franklin was skeptical that it would work at all. Alexander Hamilton wondered whether Washington should essentially be an elected monarch. Jefferson questioned the constitutionality of his own Louisiana Purchase.

Today's debates represent conflict, not crisis. Madison envisioned politics in America as a great public square where ideas competed for favor. Conflict is at the core of our politics, and the Constitution is designed to manage it. There have been few debates in American history more fundamental—and more fierce—than the internal debates the framers had about the Constitution. For better or for worse—and I would argue that it is for better—the Constitution allows and even encourages

TEA PARTY PROTESTS HAVE BROUGHT A NEW FOCUS ON THE CONSTITUTION deep arguments about the most basic democratic issues. A crisis is when the Constitution breaks down. We're not in danger of that. A crisis is when the Constitution is ignored. And we're not in danger of that either.

Nor are we in danger of flipping the Constitution on its head, as some of the Tea Party faithful contend. Their view of the founding documents was pretty well summarized by Texas Congressman and presidential candidate Ron Paul back in 2008: "The Constitution was written explicitly for one purpose—to restrain the federal government." Well, not exactly. In fact, the framers did something a little different: They created the federal government. They strengthened the center and weakened the states. The states had extraordinary power under the Articles of Confederation. Most of them had their own navies and their own currencies. The truth is, the Constitution massively strengthened the central government of the U.S. for the simple reason that it established one where none had existed before.

The Constitution did not so much limit the federal government as it created a federal government of limited powers. Even so, those powers are pretty vast. Article I, Section 8, the longest section of the longest article of the Constitution, is a drumroll of congressional power. And it ends with the "necessary and proper" clause, which delegates to Congress the power "to make all laws which shall be necessary and proper for carrying into Execution the foregoing Powers, and all other powers vested by this Constitution in the Government of the United States, or in any Department or Officer thereof." That's pretty darn open-ended.

But it is a central government with defined and limited powers. It is a central government with checks and balances that restrain the power of each of the government's three branches. It plays off power against power. In creating a central government, the framers spent as much time figuring out how to limit it as to give it power. It is true that the framers, like Tea Partyers, feared concentrated central power more than disorder. They were, after all, revolutionaries. To them, an all-powerful state was a greater threat to liberty than was discord and turbulence. Jefferson, like many of the antifederalists, thought the Constitution created too much centralized power. (Though not one of the framers—during the Constitutional Convention he was away in Paris serving as American Minster to France—he had decided opinions on the document they produced.) Most of all, the framers created a weak Executive because they feared kings. They created checks and balances to neutralize any concentration of power. This often makes for disorderly government, but it does forestall any one branch from having too much influence. The fram-

"THE CONSTITUTION DID NOT SO MUCH LIMIT THE FEDERAL GOVERNMENT AS IT CREATED A FEDERAL GOVERNMENT OF LIMITED POWERS."

ers weren't afraid of a little messiness. Which is another reason we shouldn't be so delicate about changing the Constitution or reinterpreting it. It was written in a spirit of change and revolution and turbulence. It was not written in stone. Its purpose was to create a government that could unite and lead and govern a new nation, a nation the framers hoped would grow in size and strength in ways they could not imagine. And it did.

I would argue they crated a document that spells out certain enduring principles. How those principles apply is up to each new generation to figure out. Each generation faces its own set of issues that call for constitutional interpretation. The civil rights movement brought up profound constitutional issues. So did the Korean War. So did Watergate. So did dozens of other national events. Today, a whole new set of events is causing constitutional debate. Some news events have a way of triggering instantaneous constitutional sparring: the rise of WikiLeaks fueled the debate over the limits to free speech; the shooting of Representative Gabrielle Giffords did the same for the right to bear arms. But a number of other issues in the news lately have deep constitutional subcurrents. Let's look at five that raised constitutional questions: the requirement on health insurers to cover contraception, the military action in Libya, the debt ceiling, Obamacare, and immigration.

1. Contraception Coverage

Congress shall make no law respecting an establishment of religion, or prohibiting the free exercise thereof.

– FIRST AMENDMENT

Madison did not believe in the complete separation of church and state (the phrase comes from Jefferson), but as he said many times, each will be stronger "the less they are mixed together." Any and all religious views can exist in Madison's great public square, but government cannot tip its hand one way or another. Government shouldn't be in the position of advancing or abasing religion—but few if any of the framers would have said that a politician's personal religious views shouldn't influence his actions.

The Obama administration regulation requiring religious organizations that provide health care insurance to their employees to cover contraception elicited cries of protest from people who say the administration is abridging religious liberty and violating the conscience of Catholics, that the White House is waging war on religious freedom and the First Amendment. Some on the far right even argue that Obama wants to purge religion, specifically Christianity, from the public square.

For the most part, the framers were not models of religious devotion. In fact, none of the first five presidents was particularly religious. Jefferson was a Deist, and to today's evangelical Christians, that's almost like being an unbeliever. In writing the First Amendment, the framers were reacting to the heavy hand of state religion in England, where the King was not only head of state but head of the church. The First Amendment says that government cannot favor one religion over another, nor can it disfavor any faith. Basically, it says that the government should remain neutral in the face of religion and give religious organizations pretty much complete freedom in conducting their own affairs. Government shouldn't impede religion but it shouldn't necessarily promote it either.

It seems pretty clear from Supreme Court decisions going all the way back to an 1878 decision saying that polygamy in the Mormon church was not constitutionally protected that religious organizations and in-

A PROTEST OVER WHITE HOUSE POLICY
ON INSURANCE COVERAGE FOR CONTRACEPTION

dividuals have to abide by the law even if it sometimes gets in the way of religious exercise. In a 1982 Supreme Court case about an Amish employer who refused to withhold Social Security taxes, the Court ruled, "not all burdens on religion are unconstitutional. The state may justify a limitation on religious liberty by showing that it is essential to accomplish an overriding governmental interest." In other words, the common interest and the general law trumps the special interest of a particular religious group. The idea here is that laws apply across the board. You cannot pick and choose which to follow based on your religious beliefs. In a 1990 case involving two Native Americans in Oregon who said the use of peyote, though ordinarily against the law in their state, was a part of their religion, the Court said, "To make an individual's obligation to obey such a law contingent upon the law's coincidence with his religious beliefs ... permitting him, by virtue of his beliefs, 'to become a law unto himself,' contradicts both constitutional tradition and common sense."

In the case of the Obama administration's regulations, it doesn't seem like a giant infringement of religious principles. Many Catholic employers were already providing medical insurance for contraception—and, according to polls, the great majority of Catholic women use or have used some sort of contraception—and support its availability. The regulation certainly does not impede the right to worship or the free exercise of one's religious faith. But at the same time, it doesn't make a whole lot of sense to be insensitive to people's religious beliefs. For decades, government and the courts have tried to carve out sensible exceptions for religious groups and it probably would have behooved the Obama administration to consult with Catholic authorities before going ahead with the regulations and then having to trim them back.

2. Libya

'The Congress shall have Power ... To declare War.'

ARTICLE I, SECTION 8

'The president shall be Commander in Chief of the Army and Navy of the United States.'

ARTICLE II, SECTION 2

AMERICA'S INVOLVEMENT IN LIBYA IN 2011
LED TO DISAGREEMENTS OVER PRESIDENTIAL WAR POWERS

After President Obama launched military action in Libya, Speaker of the House John Boehner asserted that the president was in violation of the War Powers Resolution. That resolution, passed in 1973, requires the President to withdraw U.S. forces from armed hostilities if Congress has not given its approval within 60 days. The Administration argued that what the U.S. was doing in Libya did not meet the threshold of hostilities in the legislation, so the resolution did not apply.

Let's be honest. No president wants to have his powers as Commander in Chief curtailed. Presidents basically say, I'm the commander in chief, and my duty is to protect and defend the U.S., and I can't be tied down by congressional foot-dragging or posturing on C-SPAN. When it comes to presidential Executive power, where you stand is where you sit. And if you're sitting in the Oval Office, presidential power looks pretty good. All Presidents—regardless of party—tend to have expansive views of Executive power. And pretty much every presidential candidate, including then-Senator Obama, criticizes the sitting president for overreaching. Candidate Obama supported the War Powers Resolution. In 2007 he said, "The President does not have power under the Constitution to unilaterally authorize a military attack in a situation that does not involve stopping an actual or imminent threat to the nation." When it comes to being commander in chief, presidents have a lot more in common with one another than with whatever their own party says when it is out of power.

Since the signing of the Constitution in 1787, Congress has declared war exactly five times: the War of 1812, the Mexican War, the Spanish-American War, and World Wars I and II. And since 1787, Presidents have put U.S. military forces into action hundreds of times without congressional authorization. The most intense of these actions was the Korean War, to which President Harry Truman sent some 1.8 million soldiers, sailors, and airmen over a period of just three years. Some 36,000 lost their lives, but Truman never sought or received a congressional declaration of war. Congress has not declared war since World War II, despite there having been dozens of conflicts since then.

The War Powers Resolution was meant to counteract what Richard Nixon, and Lyndon Johnson before him, had done in Vietnam. Congress felt manipulated and deceived and wanted to affirm its power as the war-declaring body. But the resolution is not exactly a macho assertion of congressional prerogative. It politely asks for an authorization letter and then gives the president a three-month deadline. Yet since 1973, presidents have at best paid it lip service. Presidents of both parties have used military force without prior approval from Congress—for example, in Libya in 1986, Panama in 1989, Somalia in 1992, Bosnia in 1995, and Kosovo in 1999. But in an age of potential nuclear war, global terrorism, and missiles that can be launched in seconds and take only minutes to travel thousands of miles, the president must be able to act quickly. In 1787 it took months to order uniforms and muster troops—and declarations of war were written on parchment with quill pens.

It seems clear that when it came to Libya, Obama did not adhere to the spirit of the War Powers Resolution. He did not ask for authorization, even though he probably would have had congressional support in March 2011. The White House argued that the operations did not involve "sustained fighting or active exchanges of fire with hostile forces, nor do they involve U.S. ground troops." In short, the administration said, You call this a war? We're not even the lead dog.

The question is, do Americans really want to let Congress have the sole power to commit U.S. forces to action? The law permits the President to act unilaterally, at least for the first 60 to 90 days. But Congress was trying to have it both ways: It wanted to reassert its primacy, but wasn't sure whether it really wanted to end the action in Libya. If it did, lawmakers had one very clear power that could have stopped the action overnight: They could defund it.

This is all part of the cat-and-mouse game of checks and balances. The War Powers Resolution is a check on presidential power, but the president seeks to balance this by, well, ignoring it. That's not unconstitutional; that's how our system works. The larger question is whether the War Powers Resolution is constitutional. And the Constitution is in conflict with itself here: the commander-in-chief clause vs. the Congress-must-declare-war clause. There's a lot of white space between these two assertions. Republicans were questioning Obama's use of Executive power. But the greatest proponent of Executive power in modern times was George W. Bush. In fact, it was John Yoo, Deputy Assistant Attorney General in the Office of Legal Counsel for Bush, who wrote that when it came to Bush's role as Commander in Chief, there were "no limits on the Executive's judgment." And, of course, candidate Obama was very critical of that.

Despite the fact that 10 Congressmen, including Ron Paul and Dennis Kucinich, sued the President for violating the War Powers Resolution, the matter did not end up in the Supreme Court. Congress does not really want the responsibility of deciding whether to send troops to places like Libya. It just doesn't want the president to do so in a way that makes it look superfluous and impotent.

THE FIGHT OVER THE U.S. DEBT CEILING RAISED QUESTIONS ABOUT THE
CONSTITUTIONAL OBLIGATION OF THE U.S. TO SATISFY ITS LENDERS

3. The Debt Ceiling

'The Congress shall have power ...
To borrow money on the credit of the United States.'
ARTICLE I, SECTION 8

'The validity of the public debt
of the United States ... shall not be questioned.'
14TH AMENDMENT, SECTION 4

No one disputes that Congress has the power to tax. That's one of
the very first of the enumerated powers in the Constitution. The framers
created a central government in part to be able to pay off the debts from
the Revolutionary War. The country was broke. You might not like the
power to tax, but it is one of the basic tenets of representative government. The Boston Tea Party slogan was "No taxation without representation." It wasn't "No taxation."

During the fight over raising the federal debt ceiling in the summer
of 2011, there were those in Congress and beyond who suggested that if

the U.S. did not raise the debt ceiling and instead defaulted, it would be a lesson to a spendthrift government not to borrow more than it can repay. But the idea that we can default on our debt is not only reckless; it's probably unconstitutional. No one is saying the debt is wise and prudent—far from it—but defaulting on it flies in the face of one of the few absolute proscriptions in the Constitution, Section 4 of the 14th Amendment: "The validity of the public debt ... shall not be questioned." The idea is that the U.S. shouldn't weasel out of its debts. It does not say that we can't undertake dumb obligations—the Constitution can't prevent bridges to nowhere—but that we need to pay off the public obligations that we do set for ourselves, whether those are Social Security payments to retirees or interest to Chinese bankers. When Congress borrows money "on the credit of the United States," it creates a binding obligation to pay that debt.

The debate over raising the debt ceiling was mostly cable-TV playacting. The party out of power is almost always against raising the debt limit, and the party in power is almost always for it. When Bush needed to raise the debt limit in 2006, then Senators Obama and Joe Biden voted against it, with Obama saying that raising the limit was "a sign of leadership failure." Since 1962, Congress has enacted 75 separate measures to alter the limit on the debt, including 17 under Ronald Reagan, six under Jimmy Carter and four under Bill Clinton. Congress has raised the debt limit 10 times since 2001. It ain't a partisan issue.

At the same time, there's nothing unconstitutional about the public debt's exceeding the size of the GDP. It's not wise, and we might look like Greece, but it's not unconstitutional. And there's nothing unconstitutional about Congress's trying to impose cuts in the federal budget to decrease the size of the debt or to bargain for cuts in order to vote to raise the ceiling. But if in the end Congress seems intent on allowing the U.S. to default on its debt, the President can assert that that is unconstitutional and take extraordinary measures to avoid it. He can use his Executive power to order the Treasury to produce binding debt instruments that cover all of the U.S.'s obligations around the world. He can sell assets, furlough workers, freeze checks—heck, he could lease Yellowstone Park. And it would all be constitutional.

4. Obamacare

*'The Congress shall have power ... To regulate Commerce
with foreign Nations, and among the several States.'*
ARTICLE I, SECTION 8

Critics have argued that Obama's health care act takes government
power to unprecedented—and unconstitutional—levels. They contend
that the government can't compel us to do things, or buy things, simply because we are here. In his ruling declaring the Affordable Care Act
unconstitutional, Florida federal District Judge Roger Vinson argued,
"Never before has Congress required that everyone buy a product from a
private company (essentially for life) just for being alive and residing in
the United States."

Well, maybe. The government does require us to pay taxes, serve on
juries, register for the draft. The government also compels us to buy car
insurance (if we want to legally drive our car), which is a product from a
private company. George Washington once signed a bill asking Americans to buy a musket and ammunition. There's nothing in the Constitution that restricts the government from asking us to do something or
buy something or pay a tax—even if we don't like it.

No one really disputes Congress's power to regulate interstate commerce, and it's silly to argue that health care—which accounts for 17%
of the U.S. economy—doesn't involve interstate commerce. Your doctor's
stethoscope was made in one state and was shipped to and sold in another. What conservatives mostly argue is that the individual mandate
in the bill is unconstitutional and that the government can't regulate
something you don't do. Supporters of Obamacare note that it's not a
mandate but, in effect, a tax, imposed on people who do not buy health
insurance. And that it's not universal; people who are on Medicare and
Medicaid, for example, don't need that coverage.

One would like to think that the decision to buy health insurance—or
not—is a private one. If you're young and healthy, you might just say, I'd
rather spend my money on something else. That's your right—and it may
well be a rational decision. But it's hard to argue that not buying health

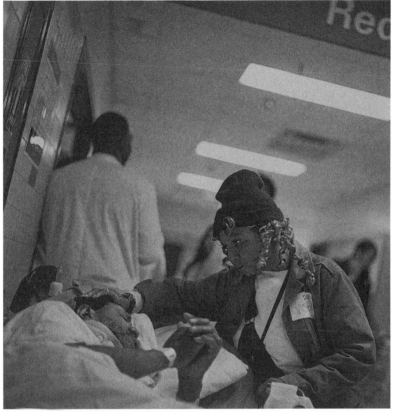

NATIONAL HEALTH CARE —DOES IT OVERSTRETCH THE POWER GRANTED TO CONGRESS BY THE CONSTITUTION TO REGULATE INTERSTATE COMMERCE?

insurance has no interstate economic consequences. Opponents say Congress can regulate commercial activity only, and not buying health insurance is not an activity—it's doing nothing.

But what happens when that healthy, young uninsured woman goes skiing and tears her anterior cruciate ligament and has to have emergency surgery? She can't afford to pay the full fee, and the hospital absorbs much of the cost. That's basically a tax on everyone who does have health insurance, and it ultimately raises the cost of hospital care and insurance premiums. I devoutly believe in Justice Louis Brandeis' famous dissent in the 1928 wiretapping case of *Olmstead* v. *United States,* in which he wrote that the Constitution conferred on all of us "the right to be let alone—the most comprehensive of rights and the right most valued by civilized men." Amen. But doing nothing can be a private decision with public consequences. Some argue that the Affordable Care Act is cynical. As a University of Pennsylvania Law Review article contended, "Making healthy young adults pay billions of dollars in premiums into the national health-care market is the only way to fund universal coverage without raising substantial new taxes." But cynicism—or pragmatism—is not proscribed by the Constitution. The Affordable Care Act may be bad legislation, as some contend, but that doesn't mean it's unconstitutional. There's no law against bad laws. The remedy for bad laws is elections.

5. Immigration

'All persons born or naturalized in the United States,
and subject to the jurisdiction thereof, are citizens
of the United States and of the State wherein they reside.'

14TH AMENDMENT, 1868

All around the world, there are basically three ways of acquiring citizenship: by birth, by blood, or by naturalization. All of them depend on the circumstances of one's birth. The principle of *jus soli* (right of the soil) means that if you're born within the borders of a country, you're automatically a citizen. *Jus sanguinis* (right of blood) means that if your parents are citizens of a country, you too are a citizen, no matter where you were born. And naturalization is the process by which a noncitizen becomes a citizen through residency, a test, or an oath—or some combination of the three.

The U.S. is one of the last nations—and by far the largest—to follow the principle of *jus soli,* better known as birthright citizenship. The 14th Amendment, ratified in 1868, basically holds that if you're physically born in the U.S. or a U.S. territory, you're a citizen. Full stop. Of the world's advanced economies, only the U.S. and Canada offer birthright

IMMIGRANTS SCALE A FENCE DIVIDING MEXICO AND ARIZONA

citizenship. No European nation does so. Nor does China or Japan. We are in part a jus sanguinis nation as well, in that children of American citizens who are born outside the U.S. can become citizens. But in the latter case, it's not so simple. For example, an out-of-wedlock child born to an unemployed illegal-immigrant mother in Paris, Texas, is a citizen when he breathes his first breath, whereas a child born to an American mother and father working for IBM in Paris, France, must apply for a certificate of citizenship and file months or years of paperwork with the State Department to show evidence that the child qualifies for American citizenship. Last year nearly 620,000 immigrants went through the naturalization process in the U.S., which on top of the paperwork includes tests in English and civics that many *jus soli* citizens might not be able to pass.

It was the 14th Amendment, one of the post–Civil War Reconstruction amendments, that made it crystal clear that anyone born in the U.S. was a citizen. It was passed for a very specific reason: to establish that former slaves were indeed citizens and entitled to all the rights of citizenship, including voting. For African Americans, this was a new birth of freedom. The 14th Amendment was a reaction to the Supreme Court's infamous Dred Scott decision of 1857, which asserted that African Americans were "beings of an inferior order" who "had no rights which the white man was bound to respect." That ruling declared that African Americans could never be U.S. citizens and were therefore not entitled to any constitutional protections. The 14th Amendment reversed that. In drafting the 14th Amendment, Congress was definitely not thinking about illegal immigration. At the time, the country needed a lot more immigrants, legal or otherwise. Congress was thinking more practically. It wanted to ensure former slaves the vote so that white Southern Democrats would not try to reverse the gains of the Civil War. It was also a direct response to the Black Codes passed by Southern states that sought to put freed slaves into something like the condition they were in before the war.

Some opponents of birthright citizenship argue that illegal immigrants are not under U.S. jurisdiction and therefore their children should not automatically become citizens, but this argument doesn't hold up under scrutiny. Senator Lindsey Graham of South Carolina has suggested he might offer an amendment to overturn the principle of birthright citizenship. I've always thought it odd that a nation united not by blood or religion or ethnic identity but by certain extraordinary ideas is a nation where citizenship is conferred on the basis of where you were physically born. It's equally strange to me that a nation that was forged through immigration—and is still formed by immigration—is also a nation that makes it constitutionally impossible for someone who was not physically born here to run for president. (Yes, the framers had their reasons for that, but those reasons have long since vanished.)

Critics of birthright citizenship argue that people come here to give birth—and some do—and that the U.S. has a rash of anchor babies who then get all kinds of rights for their families. But the law says the parents of such a child must wait until she is 21 for her to be allowed to sponsor them to live and work legally in the U.S., and research shows that the vast majority of children of illegal immigrants are born years after the mother and father have arrived in the U.S.

But even so, it's a problem.

There are liberals and conservatives alike who oppose changing birthright citizenship. It's seen as a core American value. It is important to African Americans as well as Hispanic Americans. But it is an outmoded law. However, changing the birthright-citizenship law would not end immigration or even slow it. Most illegal immigrants are economic immigrants.

Arizona and Georgia have passed laws designed to decrease illegal immigration by making it a crime for illegal immigrants not to carry documentation and by giving the police broad powers to detain anyone suspected of being in the country illegally without such documents. A federal district court struck down certain provisions in the Arizona bill.

There may well be parts of these bills that are unconstitutional, but it's unclear what the rights of illegal immigrants are, as opposed to those of citizens. The U.S. needs to take a carrot-and-stick approach to illegal immigration. Many progressives and business leaders agree that we need to make legal immigration easier, grant legal status to undocumented young people who enter college or join the military, and staple a green card to every engineering degree earned by a foreign-born national. That's the carrot. The stick is that we need better workplace enforcement, a reasonable standard for policing, and more secure borders. We need to make legal immigration easier, faster, and cheaper so that illegal immigration becomes harder and less desirable.

There is an old Latin phrase, *inter arma enim silent leges,* which roughly translates as "in time of war, the law is silent." But it's not just in times of war that the Constitution is silent. The Constitution is silent much of the time. And that's a good thing. Two hundred twenty-five years after it was written, the Constitution is more a guardrail for our society than a traffic cop. It works so well precisely because it is so opaque, so general, so open to various interpretations. Originalists contend that the Constitution has a clear, fixed meaning. But the framers argued vehemently about its meaning. For them, it was a set of enduring principles, not a code of laws. A code of laws says you have to stop at the red light; a constitution has broad principles that are unchanging but that must accommodate each new generation and circumstance.

We can pat ourselves on the back about the past 225 years, but we cannot let the Constitution become an obstacle to the U.S.'s moving into the future with a sensible health care system, a globalized economy, an evolving sense of civil and political rights. The Constitution, as Martin Luther King Jr. said in his great speech on the Mall, is a promissory note. That note had not been fulfilled for African Americans. But I would say the Constitution remains a promissory note, one in which "We the People" in each generation try to create that more perfect union.

A constitution in and of itself guarantees nothing. Bolshevik Russia had a constitution, as did Nazi Germany. Cuba and Libya have constitutions. A constitution must embody something that is in the hearts of the people. In the midst of World War II, the great judge Learned Hand gave a speech in New York City's Central Park that came to be known as "The Spirit of Liberty." It was a dark time, with freedom and liberty under threat in Europe. Hand noted that we are Americans by choice, not birth. That we are Americans precisely because we seek liberty and freedom—not only freedom from oppression but freedom of speech and belief and action. "What do we mean when we say that first of all we seek liberty?" he asked. "I often wonder whether we do not rest our hopes too much upon constitutions, upon laws and upon courts. These are false hopes; believe me, these are false hopes. Liberty lies in the hearts of men and women; when it dies there, no constitution, no law, no court can even do much to help it."

The Constitution does not protect our spirit of liberty; our spirit of liberty protects the Constitution. The Constitution serves the nation; the nation does not serve the Constitution.

That's what the framers would say.

AT THE NATIONAL ARCHIVES
IN WASHINGTON, D.C. A
GUARD STANDS BY AN
ORIGINAL COPY OF THE
CONSTITUTION

The Anchor Of Our Republic

By Michael W. McConnell

THE CONSTITUTION OF THE UNITED STATES IS GETTING QUITE a workout these days. With an undeclared war in Libya, recess appointments without a recess, judicial override of a referendum disapproving same-sex marriage, GPS devices attached to cars without a warrant, and controversy over whether Congress can compel all Americans to purchase health insurance, this 225-year-old document is being called upon to guide us through a confounding new world.

Some say it isn't up to the task.

So different is our world today that the framers of the Constitution would not have a clue what half of our cases are even about. What's a GPS? A drone attack? Health insurance? James Madison would be scratching his head in perplexity. Even if the subject matter were understandable, why should we be governed by values and principles of men who lived so long ago?

You might expect skeptics of the Constitution to conclude that since the Constitution is outmoded and unclear, questions about same-sex marriage, abortion, or school prayer should be left to the voters and their elected representatives to decide. You would be wrong. Instead they

Michael W. McConnell, a senior fellow at the Hoover Institute, is a professor of law and director of the Constitutional Law Center at Stanford University. He was formerly a judge on the U.S. Court of Appeals for the Tenth Circuit.

argue that judges, and in particular the nine justices of the Supreme Court, should "update" the Constitution for us. These skeptics disbelieve in the actual Constitution, but wish to be governed by unelected judges in the name of a "living Constitution" never adopted by the People of the United States.

But from the other end of the spectrum has emerged a great ground-swell of devoted attention to the Constitution, shaped by the conviction that if our leaders read the document closely and abided by it, most of our national problems would be solved. If only it were that easy.

Let's recall some fundamentals.

The Constitution establishes a republican form of government, speci-fying the ground rules for our political system: allocation of representative power, terms for elected officials, the electoral college, rules for appoint-ment of other officers, presidential vetoes and congressional overrides, and so forth. These provisions create the framework in which democratic politics proceeds. To play democratic politics without a Constitution would be like playing football without a rulebook. The basic law of a dem-ocratic system cannot be up for grabs in the midst of every political crisis.

Look what happens in a country without a fixed and binding consti-tution, when a Vladimir Putin or a Hugo Chávez refuses to relinquish power at the end of his term, or critics of the Iranian regime wake up in nasty prisons, or elections are rigged in Zimbabwe. The people have no agreed-upon legal basis for challenging such actions.

The framers who met in Philadelphia in 1787 created a powerful new federal government—far more powerful than that of the Articles of Con-federation that preceded it, and more powerful than some critics of gov-ernment wish to acknowledge. Regardless of whether those powers are broad enough to compel all Americans, for example, to purchase private health insurance, they certainly are broad enough to enable the govern-ment to regulate the national economy and to preempt inconsistent state laws that would balkanize our American common market.

But the framers did not make the central government all-powerful. Its powers are listed, defined, and limited. For the most part, non-economic issues, often cultural in nature, are left to the states. This

division of authority enables different parts of the nation to preserve diverse ways of life. Utah does not have to be like California, or vice versa. Efforts to nationalize decisions over educational content, marriage law, morals legislation, and the tradeoff between state taxes and services threaten this diversity.

Most important matters are left to the democratic process for decision: war, peace, taxes, spending, debt, and regulation. Unlike some recently enacted constitutions around the world, which purport to compel action on such matters as health, education, the environment, and poverty, our Constitution entrusts such questions to democratic deliberation and vote. If our elected leaders mess up the economy, it is their fault and ours—not the Constitution's.

That is why the health care controversy excites such opposite reactions. Supporters see the government mandate that citizens must buy insurance as an ordinary exercise of policymaking in an area of undoubted importance to the economy. Opponents see it as a dangerous breach of the principle that while the government may regulate commerce, it may not force individuals to engage in commerce, by requiring them to buy insurance. What else, they ask, can the government make us buy or do? Their deeper fear is that if this law is upheld, there will be no limits.

Even within the federal government, authority is carefully dispersed among competing institutions: the House of Representatives, the Senate, the president, and the judiciary. The framers thus embedded within the powerful new federal government some internal checks against overreach. These checks and balances sometimes frustrate the quick fulfillment of political agendas (good and bad). This is often derided as "gridlock." The framers considered gridlock a feature, not a bug. They feared hasty and oppressive government action more than they feared the opposite.

Under this system, the president of the United States occupies a commanding position, but he is subordinate to the law and often forced to compromise in order accomplish his objectives. In particular, he cannot enact laws; only Congress can do that, subject to his veto. He cannot spend tax dollars on his own initiative, or borrow money on the credit of the United States without congressional approval, appoint officers to run the agencies of the federal government without Senatorial advice and consent (with a narrow exception for appointments during a recess), and he cannot start a war.

During the last few decades, both Republican and Democratic presidents have stretched and maybe even breached these limits. President George W. Bush made sweeping claims of unilateral executive authority in the national security arena and asserted the power to override congressional statutes as Commander in Chief. President Obama joined in a coalition attack on Libya without congressional authorization, and early in 2012 became the first president in history to assert the authority to make recess appointments when the Senate was formally not in recess.

Some of these constitutional controversies will reach the courts, but some (including the war) will not. For these, we rely on the power of public opinion for enforcement of constitutional limits. It helps to have an alert and constitutionally knowledgeable citizenry, and an engaged and dispassionate press.

The framers further protected against all-powerful government by listing and defining a set of rights, which no arm of the state is permitted to abridge—such as the freedoms of speech and press, petition, assembly, and religion, the right to keep and bear arms, protection against confiscation of property without payment, the guarantee of due process, and a set of procedural rights that guarantee fairness and humanity in the administration of criminal law. But the Constitution does not protect every possible right, or authorize judges to make up new ones. Many of our most precious rights—to security from private attack, to employment nondiscrimination, even against wiretapping—are primarily products of legislation, not of the Constitution itself. Some of the most controversial and damaging decisions in our nation's history have been those in which the judiciary has overstepped those bounds.

Judges in our system have two grave responsibilities: One is to uphold and enforce constitutional limits when they apply, even in the face of government power and popular opinion. The second is to stand back and allow democratic politics to govern when the Constitution is silent, even when the judge's own political preferences go the other way. The second is no less important than the first, and is often more difficult. This brings us back to the question: How can this very old Constitution possibly resolve any of the questions we have about government today?

The answer requires recognizing that the Constitution contains enduring principles of free government, and not a list of specific applications. When we face constitutional issues today, we do not ask what the framers would have done. We ask what principles they enacted, and how those principles apply to the often very different circumstances now.

For example, in 2012 the federal courts considered whether an investigative blogger is entitled to the same protections of freedom of the press as is a professional newspaper reporter. Some might throw up their hands and say, "The framers did not even know what a blogger is!" But that doesn't matter. The principle of freedom of the press applies no less to the internet than to a photocopier than to movies than to handbill distribution than to Gutenberg's invention. And the framers believed that the freedom to publish our opinions belongs to everyone—not just to professional journalists (who barely existed as a profession in 1791). Bloggers included. The framers did not know about blogging, but they understood the principle that "[t]he free communication of thoughts and opinions is one of the invaluable rights of man; and every citizen may freely speak, write, and print on any subject."

GPS devices were unknown when the Fourth Amendment was added to the Constitution in 1791. But the purpose of a warrant was to authorize officials to gain access to the "persons, houses, papers, and effects" of citizens—an act which would otherwise be an illegal trespass. We know that attaching something to a person's property without permission would have been regarded as a trespass under the common law in 1791. Applying the original principle of the Fourth Amendment to the circumstances of today, the Supreme Court had no difficulty in concluding early in 2012 that police required a warrant before they could lawfully attach a GPS to a car.

Similarly, we know that before independence, Britain's Parliament had power to decide the qualifications of ministers under the established Church of England, and that replacement of the establishment of religion by the free exercise of religion meant, among other things, that churches became free to select their own clergy. James Madison described the selection of "church functionaries" as a matter "entirely ecclesiastical." A unanimous Supreme Court was able to apply that principle in 2012 to reject a claim that anti-discrimination law prohibited a Lutheran church from firing a minister.

By the same token, in judging whether President Obama needed congressional authorization in 2011 for his actions in Libya, it matters not at all that the framers could not envision drone warfare. They distinguished between offensive and defensive wars, and between wars and mere reprisals. Before President Thomas Jefferson initiated our first foreign conflict, a naval war against the Barbary States (ironically, against Tripoli—modern day Libya), he went to Congress for authorization. Presidents have entered wars without Congress a few times in American history—most notably, in Korea and Bosnia—but these have not been our finest moments. Under our Constitution, approval by the United Nations Security Council does not substitute for an act of Congress.

There may be a few odd bits of the Constitution that no longer meet our needs. Many would jettison the electoral college (though I would not). But the Constitution's flaws are minor and its enduring principles retain their force. As the great Chief Justice John Marshall wrote: "The principles [of the Constitution] are deemed fundamental. And as the authority from which they proceed is supreme, and can seldom act, they are designed to be permanent." Dispersal of power, checks and balances, republican government, freedom of speech and religion, due process, and equal protection of the laws, to mention the most important, are just as worthy of our respect and adherence as when they were adopted.

As for the rest—all the important issues of social and economic policy the Constitution leaves to democratic government—we are free to change. We have the right to deliberate and vote, to make and repeal laws, to tax, spend, and borrow—and to bear the consequences, good and bad, of the democratic choices "We, the People" make. The Constitution is not an obstacle, it is not a cipher, and it does not change with the wind. It is the anchor of our republic.

THE PENNSYLVANIA STATEHOUSE, CIRCA 1787

... done in Convention ... the Seventeenth
Day of September in the Year of our Lord
one thousand seven hundred and Eighty seven
and of the Independence of the United States
of America the Twelfth. ARTICLE VII

The Convention: How The Deed Was Done

S OME OF THE NOTABLES INVITED TO THE CONVENTION IN
that summer of 1787 simply refused to come. One, Virginia's
Patrick Henry, said of the gathering in Philadelphia that he
"smelt a rat." Others came and found the impassioned arguments profoundly dispiriting. Even George Washington, who had
given his support early to the idea of such a gathering, watched the
debates with misgivings. In the later weeks of their discussions he
wrote to Alexander Hamilton, who had already gone back to New
York City: "I almost despair of seeing a favorable issue to the proceedings of the convention and do therefore repent having had any
agency in the business."

Actually the 55 delegates who concocted that remarkable Constitution over the course of a long, hot summer had no real mandate to do
what they did. They had gathered only to consider some possible im-
provements in the Articles of Confederation, which the 13 rebellious

colonies had agreed to in 1777 but which had clearly failed to establish an effective national government. Neither Congress nor anyone else had authorized the delegates to invent a whole new political system. That was one reason why the group decided at the start to confer in total secrecy, with the windows of the Pennsylvania statehouse shut tight and sentries stationed at the doors. When one delegate carelessly dropped a copy of a convention document, Washington began scolding, "I must entreat the gentlemen to be more careful, lest our transactions get into the newspapers and disturb the public repose."

There was very little public repose to be disturbed. The seven years of the Revolutionary War had nearly bankrupted the colonies, and both credit and currency were almost worthless. The supposedly united states quarreled fiercely over economic resources, like oyster-harvesting rights in Chesapeake Bay, and Congress had no real power to keep the peace. Then in the winter of 1786 the brief but violent Massachusetts farmers' uprising known as Shays' Rebellion had provided a garish vision of things to come.

Though it had taken Virginia's James Madison and his like-minded colleagues nearly two years to prepare the way for this "Federal Convention," the scheduled opening day, May 14, came and went without enough delegates on hand to get started. Washington's arrival the previous day was a good omen, though. Without his prestigious presence, there was little hope for any new constitution. The retired commander of the Revolutionary Army originally was a little reluctant to come, but cheering crowds hailed him all along the route from his home at Mount Vernon. In Philadelphia, Washington soon went to call on his old friend Benjamin Franklin, now 81 and gout-ridden, who traveled around Philadelphia in the city's first sedan chair, a glass-windowed Parisian creation carried by four prisoners from the Walnut Street jail. Franklin, who knew Washington's tastes well, had a cask of porter ready. Washington, Franklin, Madison—when Thomas Jefferson, then serving as Minister to Paris, read the names of all those worthies reported gathering in Philadelphia, he called them "an assembly of demigods."

They were something less than that, of course, but they were none-

THE NEED TO REVISE —OR
REPLACE —THE ARTICLES
OF CONFEDERATION HAD
BEEN MADE CLEAR BY
THE FEEBLE RESPONSE
BY CONGRESS TO SHAYS'
REBELLION, AN ARMED
REVOLT THAT ERUPTED IN
MASSACHUSETTS IN 1786.

theless an unusually admirable lot, experienced, educated, patriotic, dedicated. And though they displayed powerful individual differences in both philosophy and temperament, they showed important similarities too. Of the 55 delegates from twelve states (Rhode Island refused to participate), more than half were lawyers and eight were judges; another quarter were large landowners. All of them had held public office, 42 as Congressmen and seven as governors. And they were young. Madison, for example, was 36; Hamilton was 32. There were no women, of course, not to mention African- or Native-Americans. The new Republic that these men were to create was a republic in which slavery was still widely accepted and in which only about 10% of the inhabitants—generally white male heads of households—could vote.

When the convention finally opened in the high-ceilinged, gray-walled East Room of the Pennsylvania statehouse on a rainy Friday, May 25, the first action was to name Washington its presiding officer, a responsibility that led him to remain all but silent in the ensuing debates. He took up his position in a handsome mahogany chair ornamented with a half-sun, prompting Franklin to wonder whether it would prove to be a setting or rising sun. Many of the delegates expected Washington's fellow Virginians to provide direction. In the absence of Jefferson, the state's intellectual leadership inevitably came from "Jemmy" Madison, who was to become "the Father of the Constitution." He was shy and soft-spoken, a slender bachelor about 5 feet 6 inches tall, and, according to one account, "no bigger than a half a piece of soap." His father was a wealthy landowner (and slaveholder), and Madison never had to work for a living. He studied philosophy at the College of New Jersey (now Princeton), became an early supporter of the Revolution, helped write the Virginia constitution and won a seat in Congress. The young politician had, said a friend, "a calm expression, a penetrating blue eye—and looked like a thinking man." He studied Locke and Hume, thought deeply about political philosophy, became a protege of Jefferson's. The author of the Declaration of Independence sent him books from Paris: Voltaire, Diderot, Mirabeau. Madison sent back grafts of native American plants: pecans, cranberries.

It was typical of Madison that he had come to Philadelphia eleven days early, the first outsider there. As the opening was delayed, Madison met daily with the other Virginia delegates to work out what came to be known as the Virginia plan, a blueprint for the Constitution and thus the basic agenda for the convention. His ideas were

fairly representative of liberal opinion in his time. He was deeply suspicious of executive authority, of anything that smacked of monar-
chism. He believed profoundly in the sovereignty of the people and
in their civil rights. But he was worried that political groups tended
to divide into hostile factions, and that factions eventually led to
paralysis and chaos. The trick was somehow to bring rival forces into
equilibrium. Hence the theory of checks and balances and the separation of powers. After the convention's ceremonial opening on May 25,
the Rules Committee spent the weekend organizing its procedures,
which were formal and parliamentary—and included an important provision that no vote could prevent the delegates "from revising the subject
matter of it when they see cause." Then, although Madison had probably
drafted the Virginia plan, Governor Edmund Randolph was given the
honor of introducing it. It took him more than three hours.

The Virginia plan envisioned replacing the Confederation with a
strong national government. This government would be dominated by
a bicameral legislature elected by proportional representation (i.e., more
seats for the more populous or wealthier states). There would be a national
"executive," but the executive's only function would be to carry out the
wishes of the national legislature. This Virginian view of a powerful national government was anathema to many of the delegates. The Articles of
Confederation had promised that "Each state retains its sovereignty, freedom and independence." Indeed, when the delegates from tiny Delaware
had presented their credentials on opening day, they announced that their
state legislature had expressly forbidden them to accept any change in the
system by which each state had one vote in Congress. Delegate George
Read had asked the legislature to impose that restriction because, as he
wrote to a colleague, "such is my jealousy of most of the larger States that
I would trust nothing to their candor, generosity or ideas of public justice."

So the battle was joined on the most fundamental conflict between
the sovereign states. There were plenty of other differences—between
Northern and Southern states, commercial and agricultural states,
coastal and inland states, slave and nonslave states—but the basic issue
was the comparative voting strengths of large states and small. Most

THE SIGNING: THIS 1940 PAINTING SHOWS
WASHINGTON STANDING AT RIGHT AND A SEATED
HAMILTON LEANING TOWARDS FRANKLIN (CENTER)

of the big states demanded a powerful national government; the small ones feared coercion and insisted on states' rights. And neither side put much trust in the other. The Virginians pushed their plan through to a vote of approval within two weeks. Not only had they drafted the blueprint, but they had also created an alliance of the three most populous states, Virginia, Pennsylvania, and Massachusetts, with three Southern states that expected to grow rapidly, Georgia and the Carolinas, a sort of proto-Sunbelt. But since the rules of the convention stipulated that no preliminary votes were final, any question could be reopened, and new delegates kept arriving. New Hampshire's team came two months late, and the last Marylander only on Aug. 6.

William Paterson of New Jersey opened the small states' attack on June 9 by proposing a reconsideration of proportional representation. "New Jersey will never confederate on the plan," he declared. "She would be swallowed up. I will never consent to the present system ... Myself or my state will never submit to tyranny or despotism." The supporters of the Virginia plan were no less vehement. "Are not the citizens of Pennsylvania equal to those of New Jersey?" demanded James Wilson of Pennsylvania. "Does it require 150 of the former to balance 50 of the latter? ... If the small states will not confederate on this plan, Pennsylvania would not confederate on any other." Roger Sherman of Connecticut offered a compromise. Why, he asked on June 11, could not one chamber of the Congress have seats allotted according to population, while the other preserved the principle of one vote for each state? Eventually, of course, that was the proposal that would prevail, but Sherman's compromise met a predictable fate. The big states, having a majority, ignored it. The small states took the offensive on June 15, when Paterson presented the relatively cautious New Jersey plan. It called for a unicameral legislature of limited authority, with each state getting one vote. Others offered plans of their own. Hamilton, for example, declared that the new nation should have a kinglike executive to govern as long as he was on "good behavior." So they voted again, and the Virginians won again, by 7 to 3. And the struggle continued.

By now the heat was almost unbearable, along with the humidity and the flies. "A veritable torture during Philadelphia's hot season," wrote a French visitor, "is the innumerable flies which constantly light on the face and hands, stinging everywhere and turning everything black because of the filth they leave wherever they light." Connecticut offered Sherman's compromise a second time and a third. The Madison forces refused to budge. Madison gibed at Connecticut for tax evasion: "Has she paid, for the last two years, any money into the Continental Treasury?" Oliver Ellsworth angrily retorted, "Connecticut had more troops in the field than even the state of Virginia ... We feel the effects of it even to this day." Pennsylvania's Wilson fretfully asked why the small states persisted in their suspicions of the large ones. Gunning Bedford of Delaware provided a sharp answer: "I do not, gentlemen, trust you."

As with many battles that have long since been won, it is hard now to realize how near the delegates came to failure, an event that might have led to the breakdown of the fledgling confederation, even to the reappearance of European forces eager to recapture their lost lands. Bells rang and cannons fired for the public celebration of July 4, when many of these same men had met in this same statehouse to proclaim the Declaration of Independence eleven years earlier. But the secret debates, Washington wrote to Hamilton, "are now, if possible, in a worse train than ever; you will find but little ground on which the hope of a good establishment can be formed." Some think that compromise came only because the weather finally relented. After weeks of broiling heat, a breeze blew from the northwest on Friday, July 13. That weekend the delegates could get some sleep.

Monday the 16th was cool. The Connecticut compromise offered by Sherman a month earlier began to seem eminently reasonable. So a somewhat amended version was agreed on. From then on, things moved faster, but the long argument between the strong-government men and the states'-righters colored many other issues. It took 60 ballots before the convention could agree on how to pick a president. It voted five times to have the president appointed by Congress and voted once against that. It voted repeatedly on whether a president could be impeached and how long his term should be and whether he must be native born. The delegates also avoided settling some things, like the future of slavery. Expediently ducking the question of whether slaves were people or property, the delegates decided only that a state's voting strength should be based on the number of free citizens "and three-fifths of all other persons except Indians paying taxes."

On July 24, the convention named a five-man Committee of Detail to sort everything out and draft a coherent summary of all the votes. It gave the committee nine days to accomplish this, and then adjourned. Washington went fishing for trout. When the committee duly presented its report, the newly returned delegates began wrangling about how, if they ever got a constitution finished, it should be ratified and put into effect. With the coming of September, the framers could finally see the beginning of the end. The Pennsylvania state legislature had reconvened, and it needed the chamber where the Constitutional Convention was meeting. The dwindling collection of delegates, a dozen of whom had already gone home for one reason or another, picked a five-man Committee of Style and Arrangement to undertake the actual writing of the Constitution. Although they were not supposed to change the substance of what the convention had so far decided, it was hardly accidental that all five were strong-government advocates, and that one of them was Madison.

The actual writer was Gouverneur Morris, a one-legged but rather rakish Philadelphian who boasted what he liked to consider a muscular prose style. And prose styles do have an effect. The convention had given the committee a draft that began: "We the undersigned delegates of the States of New Hampshire, Massachusetts-bay" and so on. Morris rewrote that so it began: "We, the People of the United States..."

When the committee presented its constitution on Sept. 12, the delegates eagerly began trying to change things all over again, in ways large and small. George Mason of Virginia declared for the first time that summer that there should be a bill of rights. He was voted down, 10 states to none. Madison wanted a statement that Congress should create a national university, and Franklin wanted it authorized to dig canals, but they were both voted down too. The changing continued right up to the scheduled closing day, Sept. 17, but then it was finally time to sign. Three of the delegates present still refused, among them Virginia's Governor Randolph. The rest, however, generally subscribed to Franklin's declaration that although he too still had doubts and reservations, "I consent, sir, to this Constitution because I expect no better." He had decided that the sun on Washington's chair was rising.

Still ahead lay nine months of bitter debate before the necessary nine states ratified what had been written that summer in Philadelphia. Ahead lay the creation of the Bill of Rights. Ahead lay the Civil War, which led to the 13th Amendment, finally abolishing slavery. And the 19th Amendment declaring that women have the right to vote. But on this 17th day of September 1787, Washington wrote in his journal: "The business being closed, the members adjourned to the City Tavern, dined together and took a cordial leave of each other; after which I returned to my lodgings ... and retired to meditate on the momentous work which had been executed."

Afterwords: How the Great Debates Roared On

OF THE MAKING OF BOOKS ABOUT THE CONSTITUTION THERE is no end. But for an authentic and authoritative version of what the Constitution is about and how it got that way, you cannot beat two of the original works written on the subject: James Madison's *Notes of Debates in the Federal Convention of 1787* and *The Federalist,* by Alexander Hamilton, Madison, and John Jay. Both are currently available in paperback and e-book editions. Separately and together they tell the intertwined story of the Constitution and framers with the clear voice of the times, not the way present-day passions may choose to perceive it.

The Federalist, a series of essays churned out for New York newspapers under the group anonym "Publius," was frankly designed as propaganda and used to persuade doubters in state conventions to ratify the nascent Constitution. The pieces appeared at the rate of two to four a week. Hamilton, who hatched the idea, dashed off "Federalist No. 1" in October 1787 aboard a sloop on the Hudson and cranked out the 85th and last in May 1788, after Jay had fallen too sick to write and Madison had decamped for Virginia to fight the ratifying battle there. "Whilst the printer was putting into type parts of a number," Madison recalled, "the following parts were under the pen."

JAMES MADISON WAS ONE OF THREE AUTHORS OF *THE FEDERALIST*, A
SERIES OF ESSAYS URGING APPROVAL OF THE PROPOSED CONSTITUTION

MADISON'S CO-AUTHORS: JOHN JAY, LATER CHIEF JUSTICE OF THE SUPREME COURT, AND ALEXANDER HAMILTON, FUTURE TREASURY SECRETARY

Despite such hip-shooting urgency, *The Federalist* proved so penetrating an explication of the Constitution that 50 years later Alexis de Tocqueville described it as a tour de force that "ought to be familiar to the statesmen of all countries." Historian Marvin Meyers once called it the "most profound commentary on the original nature of the American regime, and the best single guide to the political mind of the founders."

Taken in bulk, *The Federalist* can be heavy going for the lay reader, with its sometimes intricate marshaling of closely reasoned arguments. Madison rated it "admissible as a School book if any will be that goes so much

CONTENTS.

THE

FEDERALIST:

ADDRESSED TO THE

PEOPLE OF THE STATE OF
NEW-YORK.

NUMBER I.

Introduction.

AFTER an unequivocal experience of the ineffi-
cacy of the fubfifting federal government, you
are called upon to deliberate on a new conftitution for
the United States of America. The fubject fpeaks its
own importance; comprehending in its confequences,
nothing lefs than the exiftence of the UNION, the
fafety and welfare of the parts of which it is com-
pofed, the fate of an empire, in many refpects, the
moft interefting in the world. It has been frequently
remarked, that it feems to have been referred to the
people of this country, by their conduct and example,
to decide the important queftion, whether focieties of
men are really capable or not, of eftablifhing good
government from reflection and choice, or whether
they are forever deftined to depend, for their political
conftitutions, on accident and force. If there be any
truth in the remark, the crifis, at which we are arrived,
may with propriety be regarded as the æra in which
A   that

THE OPENING PAGE OF THE FIRST EDITION OF *THE FEDERALIST,*
WHICH WAS PUBLISHED IN NEW YORK IN 1788

into detail." But the brilliance of the best individual essays remains undi-
minished. Madison's own masterly "Federalist No. 10," for example, took
issue with the perceived wisdom of his day that the government would
be threatened by the mutually hostile factions with which a sprawling
America appeared dangerously overloaded. By their very number and
variety, Madison argued, the factions would support an enduring centralized republic by canceling out one another, producing a state of bal-
anced popular will. Critics wrote off such perceptions as nonsense: No
large republic anywhere could ever survive, and as a matter of political

chemistry, a government might be either central or more loosely federal but surely not both. Madison, of course, knew otherwise, yet he sternly reminded Congress it would have an unrelenting chore ahead. "The regulation of these various and interfering interests," he wrote, "forms the principal task of modern legislation."

In "Federalist No. 78," Hamilton showed that judicial review—the right of the courts to declare a law unconstitutional—lies inherent in the Constitution, although it is stated nowhere in either the basic document or any of the amendments. Hamilton also argued for broad construction of the Constitution rather than strict adherence to its limited instructions. For nearly two centuries, the U.S. bench has tended more often to live by Hamilton's reasoning, despite frequent protests from outside the courts and even from some judges that such interpretations can intrude dangerously into legislative terrain. Hamilton stated firmly that the judiciary would "always be the least dangerous [branch] to the political rights of the Constitution."

Madison's *Notes* provides an even more eclectic guide to the minds of the founders. Ranging in length from cursory phrases to more than a dozen pages, the daily entries touch on every session of the four-month convention. "I was not absent a single day," Madison later recalled, "nor more than a cassual fraction of an hour in any day." While his memory was still fresh, he organized and transcribed the scribbles for each day. Not released until 1840, four years after the author's death, they remain the most complete and responsible record of the convention's secret debates. In quiet and elegant (if sometimes stilted) 18th-century prose, they bare the passions of every important contributor to the convention, as delegates wrestled with their own prejudices, as well as those of their colleagues, to create a lasting government. In places the brisk but resounding impact of a phrase is almost like that of Genesis, as when Madison writes that on May 29, 1787, "Mr. Randolph then opened the main business." These simple words bring onstage nothing less than the initial blueprint of the American system, a radical plan put forth by Virginia Governor Edmund Randolph for government of, by, and for the people that was, in its main outlines, much like the one the convention would approve.

IN A LETTER TO JAMES MADISON, THOMAS JEFFERSON OFFERED CRITICISMS
OF THE CONSTITUTION, ESPECIALLY "THE OMISSION OF A BILL OF RIGHTS."
IN *FEDERALIST NO. 84,* ALEXANDER HAMILTON WOULD EXPLAIN WHY THE
FRAMERS THOUGHT IT UNNECESSARY TO INCLUDE ONE

Later, with the proceedings stymied over congressional representation, Roger Sherman of Connecticut articulates a way out of the deadlock
with his famous compromise, recommending proportional state representation for the House and single delegates (later changed to two) in the
Senate. Madison, disliking anything but proportional representation
for the Senate, remains stubborn on the issue and, as a faithful and bal-
anced reporter, records his own scolding by Delaware's John Dickinson:
"You see the consequence of pushing things too far." On the explosive
matter of slavery, which many delegates deplored but sensed could not
be addressed without blowing the convention apart, Sherman observes
that the "abolition of Slavery seemed to be going on in the U.S. & that the
good sense of the several States would probably by degrees compleat it."

Throughout *Notes,* this sense of patience, common-sense accommo-
dation and compromise repeatedly rises from the pages, countering passions, defusing confrontations as most delegates strive to keep the com-
pass set on the perceived task—not to adjudicate the rights of man but to
make the government work and save the union. In so doing all were wary
of creating too strong and independent a president. "Why might not a
Cataline or a Cromwell arise in this Country as well as in others," de-
mands Pierce Butler of South Carolina. The answer: by limiting the president's power with a system of checks and balances, by keeping him under
the law that governs all other citizens of the republic, and by making him
answerable, through vote or impeachment, to his employers, the people.

Yet as *Notes* reveals, in building fences to contain the presidency, delegates wished to avoid giving offense to George Washington, who sat
among them as presiding officer of the convention and whom virtually
all assumed would head whatever government they pasted together.
"The first man put at the helm will be a good one," says Franklin, adding, "No body knows what sort may come afterwards."

Along with their priceless preservation of history, Madison's *Notes*
sparkles with the wisecracks of men enduring a marathon convention.
Franklin, having listened beyond even his own monumental patience to
arguments favoring propertied interests, comments that "Some of the
greatest rogues he was ever acquainted with, were the richest rogues."

George Mason, urging a minimum-age qualification of 25 for Congressmen, observed that "It had been said that Congress had proved a good school for our young men. It might be so for any thing he knew but if it were, he chose that they should bear the expence of their own education."

Although many scholars, jurists and politicians have since used *Notes* and *The Federalist* as evidence for their own views concerning the delegates' intentions in fashioning the Constitution, the essential value of both books is in their account of what the framers actually said and did, and what they believed they had created when finished. But even from these greatly informative texts, the intricate and full array of their intentions can never be entirely discovered or their ambiguities perfectly resolved. Madison said as much in 1796, when he bluntly declared to Congress that the framers' words or presumed thoughts at the convention "could never be regarded as the oracular guide in expounding the Constitution." But as both *The Federalist* and *Notes* make clear, if ever a document has spoken for itself, it's the U.S. Constitution.

The Constitution

A Guide to the Text

The following pages contain the
complete text of the U.S. Constitution.
It is presented in its original form,
complete with some spellings and turns of
speech that are now considered archaic.
The text is accompanied by TIME's
annotations—set in a different typeface—
that amplify, explain, and put into
historical context the language of the
document.

WE THE PEOPLE of the United States, in Order to form a more perfect Union, establish Justice, insure domestic Tranquility, provide for the common defence, promote the general Welfare, and secure the Blessings of Liberty to ourselves and our Posterity, do ordain and establish this Constitution for the United States of America.

★ The Constitution is a legal document and for the most part reads like one. But in its Preamble it reaches for civic poetry, which it unforgettably achieves. The Preamble is largely the work of one man, Gouverneur Morris, a member of the Pennsylvania delegation to the Constitutional Convention. When its deliberations were nearly complete, the Convention chose Morris as part of a five-man Committee of Style. It's job would be to produce a final draft that would put into clearer language the much amended and laboriously worded text the delegates had arrived at. That text opened with the uninspiring words, "We the People of the States of New Hampshire, Massachusetts" and so forth. Morris substituted the phrase "We the People of the United States...," affirming that authority sprang directly from the American people and emphasizing the membership of those people in a unified nation, not a mere affiliation of states. Then he went on to provide one of the most succinct statements ever set forth of the benefits of good government.

ARTICLE I

Section 1

All legislative Powers herein granted shall be vested in a Congress of the United States, which shall consist of a Senate and House of Representatives.

★ Article I lays out the powers of the legislative branch. Its first section describes the dual structure of that legislature, which was arrived at through one of the most important compromises of the Constitutional Convention. The innocuous words "herein granted" carry special meaning. They make clear that the new federal government could not claim unlimited powers but only those conferred through the Constitution.

Section 2

The House of Representatives shall be composed of Members chosen every second Year by the People of the several States, and the Electors in each State shall have the Qualifications requisite for Electors of the most numerous Branch of the State Legislature.

★ Though they considered a property requirement for voters choosing members of the House of Representatives, in the end the delegates to the Convention, the men we now call the framers, simply decided that the requirements should be whatever each state required of voters for the lower house ("the most numerous branch") of its own state legislature. What that meant in practice was that the vote was restricted at first to white males, and in most states only those with property. But in the 19th century the franchise began to expand, first by the elimination of property requirements. After the Civil War, the 15th Amendment barred the federal government or the states from denying the vote on the basis of "race, color or previous condition of servitude." And in 1920 the 19th Amendment extended the vote to women.

No Person shall be a Representative who shall not have attained to the Age of twenty five Years, and been seven Years a Citizen of the United States, and who shall not, when elected, be an Inhabitant of that State in which he shall be chosen.

★ The requirement that Representatives actually live in the state they represent was adopted to ensure that members of Congress have a real connection to the people they represent. As the framers knew, members of the British Parliament were not required to reside in the district they represented.

Representatives and direct Taxes shall be apportioned among the several States which may be included within this Union, according to their respective Numbers, which shall be determined by adding to the whole Number of free Persons, including those bound to Service for a Term of Years, and excluding Indians not taxed, three fifths of all other Persons. The actual Enumeration shall be made within three Years after the first Meeting of the Congress of the United States, and within every subsequent Term of ten Years, in such Manner as they shall by Law direct. The Number of Representatives shall not exceed one for every thirty Thousand, but each State shall have at Least one Representative; and until such enumeration shall be made, the State of New Hampshire shall be entitled to chuse three, Massachusetts eight, Rhode-Island and Providence Plantations one, Connecticut five, New-York six, New Jersey four, Pennsylvania eight, Delaware one, Maryland six, Virginia ten, North Carolina five, South Carolina five, and Georgia three.

★ This section contains the most infamous compromise arrived at by the Convention. It permitted slaves to be counted as "three fifths"

of a person for the purpose of determining the
population of a state and therefore the number
of Representatives it was entitled to send to
Congress (as well as the proportion of taxes that
each state would pay to the federal Treasury).
That slaves were referred to in the text as "all
other persons" is evidence of the unwillingness of
antislavery delegates to have slavery mentioned
explicitly in the Constitution and thereby perhaps
implicitly legitimized. Because the framers had
no clear idea of what the population of any of
the states really was, in this passage they also
established the census, calling for the first to
be held within three years, with new counts to
be made every ten. They then went on to offer a
rough estimate of how many Representatives each
state could send to the first Congress.

When vacancies happen in the Representation from any State, the
Executive Authority thereof shall issue Writs of Election to fill such
Vacancies.

The House of Representatives shall chuse their Speaker and other
Officers; and shall have the sole Power of Impeachment.

★ Though many Americans mistakenly believe
the word *impeachment* describes the trial or
even the removal of a president, "the power of
impeachment" is the power simply to bring charges,
one the Constitution grants to the House.

Section 3

The Senate of the United States shall be composed of two Senators
from each State, chosen by the Legislature thereof for six Years; and
each Senator shall have one Vote.

Immediately after they shall be assembled in Consequence of
the first Election, they shall be divided as equally as may be into
three Classes. The Seats of the Senators of the first Class shall be

vacated at the Expiration of the second Year, of the second Class at the Expiration of the fourth Year, and of the third Class at the Expiration of the sixth Year, so that one third may be chosen every second Year; and if Vacancies happen by Resignation, or otherwise, during the Recess of the Legislature of any State, the Executive thereof may make temporary Appointments until the next Meeting of the Legislature, which shall then fill such Vacancies.

No Person shall be a Senator who shall not have attained to the Age of thirty Years, and been nine Years a Citizen of the United States, and who shall not, when elected, be an Inhabitant of that State for which he shall be chosen.

★ In order to ensure that at least one branch of the legislature was not chosen directly by the people, the framers decided to have Senators selected by the legislatures of their states. And though the entire House stands for re-election every two years, the framers split the first class of Senators into three groups, each standing for re-election two years apart from the others, so that no more than a third of the Senate would face re-election every two years. That prevented a sudden turnover in what was intended to be the more stable and deliberative chamber. By the same token, while the minimum age for a Representative was set at just 25 years, Senators were required to be at least 30.

The Vice President of the United States shall be President of the Senate, but shall have no Vote, unless they be equally divided.

The Senate shall chuse their other Officers, and also a President pro tempore, in the Absence of the Vice President, or when he shall exercise the Office of President of the United States.

★ Just what is a vice president for? The framers had few ideas, other than to make him president of the Senate, but with a vote that he could only use as a tie-breaker. As George Washington's vice president, John Adams was the first man to occupy that position. He famously called it "the most insignificant office that ever the invention of man contrived or his imagination conceived."

The Senate shall have the sole Power to try all Impeachments. When sitting for that Purpose, they shall be on Oath or Affirmation. When the President of the United States is tried, the Chief Justice shall preside: And no Person shall be convicted without the Concurrence of two thirds of the Members present.

Judgment in Cases of Impeachment shall not extend further than to removal from Office, and disqualification to hold and enjoy any Office of honor, Trust or Profit under the United States: but the Party convicted shall nevertheless be liable and subject to Indictment, Trial, Judgment and Punishment, according to Law.

★ Having given the House the power to bring charges against the president, the framers empowered the Senate—the more deliberative body—to conduct the trial. And though the vice president would ordinarily preside over the Senate, the framers also decided that during impeachment trials that role should pass to the chief justice. This avoided a potential conflict of interest. Were the vice president to direct the proceedings, knowing that he would assume the Presidency in the event of a conviction, he might be tempted to issue rulings from the chair that were unfavorable to the president.

To deal with complaints that allowing the Senate to act as a court violated the separation of powers, the framers decided that political penalties—removal from office and the prohibition of holding another federal office —should be the only kind that the Senate could impose on a convicted president. Thereafter, further civil or criminal penalties could be sought against him as well, but only in a regular court of law.

Section 4

The Times, Places and Manner of holding Elections for Senators and Representatives, shall be prescribed in each State by the Legislature thereof; but the Congress may at any time by Law make or alter such Regulations, except as to the Places of chusing Senators.

The Congress shall assemble at least once in every Year, and such Meeting shall be on the first Monday in December, unless they shall by Law appoint a different Day.

★ In the early days of the republic, with many roads in poor condition and railroads still unknown, it could take months for newly elected members of Congress to make their way to Washington, D.C. Because of that, they did not assume their seats until one year after their election. The stipulation in this section that Congress should convene on the first Monday in December had this effect: In any even-numbered year when December 1 came just a few weeks after the November congressional election, Representatives from the previous Congress who already resided in Washington could continue to sit in session until the following March—including men who were retiring or had been defeated in the November elections. These lengthy "lame duck" sessions would be eliminated by the 20th Amendment in 1933, which moved the start of Congress to January 1—plenty of time, in an age of railways and good roads, for newly elected members to arrive in Washington to start their work.

Section 5

Each House shall be the Judge of the Elections, Returns and Qualifications of its own Members, and a Majority of each shall constitute a Quorum to do Business; but a smaller Number may adjourn from day to day, and may be authorized to compel the Attendance of absent Members, in such Manner, and under such Penalties as each House may provide.

Each House may determine the Rules of its Proceedings, punish its Members for disorderly Behaviour, and, with the Concurrence of two thirds, expel a Member

★ The decision by the framers to specify that each chamber of Congress would have the power to make its own rules reflects the long struggle of Parliament to assert its independence from the King. The decision to require a quorum reflects the framers' concern that a relatively small group of Representatives from states or districts close to Washington, D.C. should not be able to embark on legislative work on their own before men from more distant areas could arrive in the city.

Each House shall keep a Journal of its Proceedings, and from time to time publish the same, excepting such Parts as may in their Judgment require Secrecy; and the Yeas and Nays of the Members of either House on any question shall, at the Desire of one fifth of those Present, be entered on the Journal.

Neither House, during the Session of Congress, shall, without the Consent of the other, adjourn for more than three days, nor to any other Place than that in which the two Houses shall be sitting.

★ By the time of the Constitutional Convention in 1787, American newspapers had begun reporting on the debates and decisions of state legislatures. Though the deliberations of the House were open to the public from the time of the first Congress in 1789, the Senate chose to meet in closed session until 1794.

Section 6

The Senators and Representatives shall receive a Compensation for their Services, to be ascertained by Law, and paid out of the Treasury of the United States. They shall in all Cases, except Treason, Felony and Breach of the Peace, be privileged from Arrest during their Attendance at the Session of their respective Houses, and in going to and returning from the same; and for any Speech or Debate in either House, they shall not be questioned in any other Place.

★ As a way to prevent Congressional office from becoming an occupation that only the independently wealthy could pursue, the framers decided that members should receive a salary. (Not all agreed. Benjamin Franklin was one who thought they should serve without pay.) When the framers also gave Congressmen limited immunity from arrest when Congress is in session, their primary intention was to protect them from being arrested in civil suits—a common practice in the 18th century—or sued for slander for something said in a floor debate. But the exception made for felonies meant that Senators and Representatives could still be arrested for many crimes, including taking bribes.

No Senator or Representative shall, during the Time for which he was elected, be appointed to any civil Office under the Authority of the United States, which shall have been created, or the Emoluments whereof shall have been encreased during such time; and no Person holding any Office under the United States, shall be a Member of either House during his Continuance in Office.

★ Though the framers considered banning members of Congress from accepting any other government post, they settled instead on a more narrow ban on any post created during their time in

office, or any post for which the salary had been
increased in that time. The purpose was to prevent
members from misusing their powers of office
to create lucrative new government positions for
themselves. This clause also sought to avoid a
practice common in England, wherein members
of Parliament frequently served as ministers to
the King, a practice that violated the principle of
separation of powers among the three branches of
government.

Section 7

All Bills for raising Revenue shall originate in the House of Representatives; but the Senate may propose or concur with Amendments
as on other Bills.

★ It's notable that the framers decided that
the House, the chamber in which states were
represented in proportion to their populations (and
the one presumed to be most responsive to the
popular will) should be the place from which "bills
for raising revenue"—meaning taxes—should
originate.

Every Bill which shall have passed the House of Representatives
and the Senate, shall, before it become a Law, be presented to the
President of the United States: If he approve he shall sign it, but if
not he shall return it, with his Objections to that House in which
it shall have originated, who shall enter the Objections at large on
their Journal, and proceed to reconsider it. If after such Reconsideration two thirds of that House shall agree to pass the Bill, it shall be
sent, together with the Objections, to the other House, by which it
shall likewise be reconsidered, and if approved by two thirds of that
House, it shall become a Law. But in all such Cases the Votes of both
Houses shall be determined by Yeas and Nays, and the Names of the
Persons voting for and against the Bill shall be entered on the Journal of each House respectively. If any Bill shall not be returned by

the President within ten Days (Sundays excepted) after it shall have been presented to him, the Same shall be a Law, in like Manner as if he had signed it, unless the Congress by their Adjournment prevent its Return, in which Case it shall not be a Law.

Every Order, Resolution, or Vote to which the Concurrence of the Senate and House of Representatives may be necessary (except on a question of Adjournment) shall be presented to the President of the United States; and before the Same shall take Effect, shall be approved by him, or being disapproved by him, shall be repassed by two thirds of the Senate and House of Representatives, according to the Rules and Limitations prescribed in the Case of a Bill.

★ Though Congress is the branch of government that passes laws, the veto power effectively gives the president a role in shaping them. That's because the veto can only be overridden by a two-third majority vote, a super majority difficult to achieve: Only about 7% of presidential vetoes are successfully overridden. This gives Congress an incentive to craft laws that the president can accept, even if sometimes reluctantly.

Section 8

The Congress shall have Power To lay and collect Taxes, Duties, Imposts and Excises, to pay the Debts and provide for the common Defence and general Welfare of the United States; but all Duties, Imposts and Excises shall be uniform throughout the United States;

★ The framers were painfully aware that under the Articles of Confederation, the document that the Constitution would replace, the national government had no power to levy taxes, so they made sure to give Congress the power to do that—perhaps the most important power it was granted. But except under an emergency wartime measure during the Civil War, Congress could not tax individual incomes directly until the adoption of the 16th Amendment in 1913. Instead taxes were to be imposed on the states in proportion to their populations.

Advocates of broad government authority to promote social and economic goals often point to the clause empowering Congress to provide for the common defense and general welfare. Among the first was Alexander Hamilton, one of the framers. As George Washington's secretary of the treasury, he cited the language of this clause to justify his plan for government action to promote the growth of manufacturing—a plan that was never realized.

To borrow Money on the credit of the United States;

★ In addition to levying taxes, Congress was granted the power to borrow by various means, as it does through the sale of treasury bonds.

To regulate Commerce with foreign Nations, and among the several States, and with the Indian Tribes;

★ Under the Articles of Confederation, states were prone to impose import duties on products from other states or to make conflicting claims to authority over shared waterways. One of the main goals of the Constitution was to further the creation of a truly national economy, less burdened by such destructive competition among the states. But over time the power to regulate commerce "among the several States" was invoked not only to restrict actions by states but as a basis for significant expansions of federal authority over numerous areas of life, including laws to regulate working hours and conditions, protect the environment, provide health and safety standards as well as consumer protections, and build interstate highways. The new national health care law rests partly upon this power as well. The courts have frequently been asked to determine whether "the commerce clause" justified those exertions of federal authority. Since the late 1930s, when the Supreme Court reversed course to approve various elements of Franklin Delano Roosevelt's "New Deal," they have tended to support a broad reading of the clause. But in recent years conservatives on the Court have attempted to place limits on the powers the federal government can claim though its use.

To establish an uniform Rule of Naturalization, and uniform Laws on the subject of Bankruptcies throughout the United States;

★ The naturalization clause empowers Congress to establish rules by which immigrants can become citizens of the United States.

To coin Money, regulate the Value thereof, and of foreign Coin, and fix the Standard of Weights and Measures;
To provide for the Punishment of counterfeiting the Securities and current Coin of the United States;

★ Under the Articles of Confederation, Americans were confronted by a baffling array of currencies issued by the various states as well as foreign coins and banknotes that circulated freely. As another way to unify the nation, the framers gave Congress the power to issue a uniform national currency and the power to standardize weights and measures.

To establish Post Offices and post Roads;

★ A well operating postal system was another important aspect of a unified national economy. One of the framers had a particularly strong understanding of the importance of good postal service: Benjamin Franklin had been postmaster general for the Colonies.

To promote the Progress of Science and useful Arts, by securing for limited Times to Authors and Inventors the exclusive Right to their respective Writings and Discoveries;

★ As another means to promote economic growth, by ensuring to inventors and writers intellectual property rights, Congress was given the power to issue patents and trademarks.

To constitute Tribunals inferior to the supreme Court;

★ The framers established the Supreme Court in Article III of the Constitution, but they gave Congress the power to set up a system of lower courts, which it would do in the Judiciary Act of 1789.

To define and punish Piracies and Felonies committed on the high Seas, and Offences against the Law of Nations;

★ This clause would turn out to be important in establishing the power of Congress to make rules for dealing with modern terrorists.

To declare War, grant Letters of Marque and Reprisal, and make Rules concerning Captures on Land and Water;

★ Congress has issued just five formal declarations of war: The War of 1812, The Mexican War, the Spanish-American War, and World Wars I and II. Since the end of World War II in particular, the war power of Congress has put it frequently in conflict with the president. The Korean War, Vietnam, both Gulf Wars, and the war in Afghanistan were launched and pursued without a formal declaration by Congress, as well as numerous more limited military actions in places including the Dominican Republic, Panama, Iran, Lebanon, Grenada, Somalia, Bosnia, Kosovo, and Libya. In 1973 Congress adopted the War Powers Resolution, over the veto of President Nixon. It requires the president to withdraw U.S. forces from combat if Congress does not give him its approval within 60 days, but presidents of both parties have successfully evaded it.

To raise and support Armies, but no Appropriation of Money to that Use shall be for a longer Term than two Years;

To provide and maintain a Navy;

To make Rules for the Government and Regulation of the land and naval Forces;

★ The two-year limit on army appropriations was meant to discourage the establishment of a standing military, which many antifederalists feared could become an instrument of despotic power. The biannual appropriation power also means that if it wished to, Congress could end a war it objected to by refusing to approve funding, something it has sometimes threatened but rarely done.

To provide for calling forth the Militia to execute the Laws of the Union, suppress Insurrections and repel Invasions;

★ One of the developments that convinced many Americans that the Articles of Confederation provided an insufficient framework for governing the new nation was Shays' Rebellion, an armed uprising of debt-ridden Massachusetts farmers and laborers that began in the summer of 1786. Under the Articles, Congress was powerless to dispatch a militia to put down the rebels, a problem this clause was designed to remedy.

To provide for organizing, arming, and disciplining, the Militia, and for governing such Part of them as may be employed in the Service of the United States, reserving to the States respectively, the Appointment of the Officers, and the Authority of training the Militia according to the discipline prescribed by Congress;

★ During the Revolutionary War, militias had served alongside the Continental Army, but they were often poorly trained. (George Washington, commander of the Army, was particularly unimpressed.) The framers hoped that federal oversight would lead to more professional militias, but they left the states an important role.

To exercise exclusive Legislation in all Cases whatsoever, over such District (not exceeding ten Miles square) as may, by Cession of particular States, and the Acceptance of Congress, become the Seat of the Government of the United States, and to exercise like Authority over all Places purchased by the Consent of the Legislature of the State in which the Same shall be, for the Erection of Forts, Magazines, Arsenals, dock-Yards, and other needful Buildings; And

★ The wording of this clause leaves open the possibility that the nation's capital—which was New York City in 1787—might remain there (or move to some other city; Philadelphia being the likely alternative) or that it might eventually be located in a new ten square mile district in a still undetermined location. In this clause the framers gave Congress authority over that district should it be the option chosen. It would indeed be the one agreed upon in 1790, during George Washington's first term as president, thus creating the District of Columbia.

To make all Laws which shall be necessary and proper for carrying into Execution the foregoing Powers, and all other Powers vested by this Constitution in the Government of the United States, or in any Department or Officer thereof.

★ The "necessary and proper" clause would become one of the most powerful and contested phrases in the Constitution, a source of constant friction between those favoring broad federal powers—"implied powers"—and the supporters of more limited government. During Washington's first term, his Treasury Secretary Alexander Hamilton would publish an influential defense of the government's power to create a national bank—one that would help it fulfill its enumerated powers to collect taxes, spend for the general welfare, and support armies—that rested in large part on his expansive reading of that clause. Thomas Jefferson would argue that the clause did no more than give the government authority to take steps "absolutely necessary" to fulfill the "enumerated powers" specifically assigned to it in other parts of the Constitution — and that the bank was neither specified in the Constitution nor necessary for Congress to fulfill its enumerated powers. Washington took Hamilton's side, however, and the bank was established.

In a pivotal Supreme Court decision of 1819, *McCulloch* v. *Maryland,* Chief Justice John Marshall used Hamilton's "necessary and proper" reasoning to support the constitutionality of the Second Bank of the United States, the successor to Hamilton's bank. In words that firmly established the line of court doctrine that future justices would use to support a broad exercise of federal power, Marshall wrote: "Let the end be legitimate, let it be within the scope of the Constitution, and all means which are appropriate, which are plainly adapted to that end, which are not prohibited, but consistent with the letter and spirit of the Constitution, are constitutional."

Section 9

The Migration or Importation of such Persons as any of the States now existing shall think proper to admit, shall not be prohibited by the Congress prior to the Year one thousand eight hundred and eight, but a Tax or duty may be imposed on such Importation, not exceeding ten dollars for each Person.

★ "Such persons." Those words are yet another of the framers attempts to avoid direct mention of slavery. The decision that Congress should be forbidden to take steps earlier than 1808 to interfere with the slave trade was undertaken largely to satisfy Georgia and South Carolina. (An import ban was no threat to states of the Upper South like Virginia, which had been settled for a longer time and considered themselves already to have enough slaves.) In 1807 Congress did indeed pass legislation to end the trade the following year, after some 200,000 new slaves had arrived in the previous 20 years.

The Privilege of the Writ of Habeas Corpus shall not be suspended, unless when in Cases of Rebellion or Invasion the public Safety may require it.

★ One of the most venerable rights in English common law, habeas corpus dates back at least to the Magna Carta in 1215. It ensures that government authorities cannot hold indefinitely any person who has been arrested or otherwise detained—for instance, in a mental hospital— without satisfying a judge that the detention is lawful. That the framers identified possible exceptions to the writ in a part of the Constitution that outlines the powers of Congress implies they assumed Congress should be the branch of government authorized to suspend it. But the most famous suspensions have been undertaken by presidents. During the Civil War Abraham Lincoln suspended it for Confederate sympathizers, a controversial emergency measure that Congress later approved. As part of the war on terror that followed the attacks of 9/11, George W. Bush sought to strip "enemy combatants" of their habeas rights, a move also supported by acts of Congress. Though the Supreme Court ruled twice that detainees at the military prison at Guantanamo Bay, Cuba, had such rights, the question continued to be contested in lower courts.

No Bill of Attainder or ex post facto Law shall be passed.

★ These are other protections rooted in English common law. A bill of attainder was an act of Parliament that attempted to punish an individual or a group without trial. An ex post facto law was one passed by Parliament to punish individuals by retroactively criminalizing an action they undertook when it was not a crime.

No Capitation, or other direct, Tax shall be laid, unless in Proportion to the Census or Enumeration herein before directed to be taken.

No Tax or Duty shall be laid on Articles exported from any State.

★ The ban on export taxes was designed to protect Southern agricultural exports like tobacco, rice, and indigo. Southern states were also intent on blocking any future opportunity for non-slave states to impose an export tax that would in effect be a penalty on crops produced by slave labor, making them more expensive on world markets.

No Preference shall be given by any Regulation of Commerce or Revenue to the Ports of one State over those of another; nor shall Vessels bound to, or from, one State, be obliged to enter, clear, or pay Duties in another.

★ This provision ensured that Congress would not favor one state over another in the matter of regulating ocean-going commerce or commerce by interior waterways.

No Money shall be drawn from the Treasury, but in Consequence of Appropriations made by Law; and a regular Statement and Account of the Receipts and Expenditures of all public Money shall be published from time to time.

★ Here the framers sought to guarantee transparency in the Congressional budget process.

No Title of Nobility shall be granted by the United States: And no Person holding any Office of Profit or Trust under them, shall, without the Consent of the Congress, accept of any present, Emolument, Office, or Title, of any kind whatever, from any King, Prince, or foreign State.

★ Having won a War of Independence against Great Britain, a nation with a hereditary aristocracy, the framers were intent on discouraging the growth of such a thing on American soil.

Section 10
No State shall enter into any Treaty, Alliance, or Confederation; grant Letters of Marque and Reprisal; coin Money; emit Bills of Credit; make any Thing but gold and silver Coin a Tender in Payment of Debts; pass any Bill of Attainder, ex post facto Law, or Law impairing the Obligation of Contracts, or grant any Title of Nobility.

★ After spelling out the powers of Congress, the
Constitution in this section makes explicit various
powers denied to the states. The prohibition on
coining money, issuing bills of credit, or accepting
as legal tender anything other than gold or silver
reflects the framers determination to end the
practice by some states of issuing debased paper
currency.

No State shall, without the Consent of the Congress, lay any Imposts or Duties on Imports or Exports, except what may be absolutely necessary for executing its inspection Laws: and the net Produce
of all Duties and Imposts, laid by any State on Imports or Exports,
shall be for the Use of the Treasury of the United States; and all such
Laws shall be subject to the Revision and Controul of the Congress.

No State shall, without the Consent of Congress, lay any Duty of
Tonnage, keep Troops, or Ships of War in time of Peace, enter into
any Agreement or Compact with another State, or with a foreign
Power, or engage in War, unless actually invaded, or in such imminent Danger as will not admit of delay.

★ Though states already had their own militias to
keep order within their own borders, here the
framers acted to prevent them from forming
standing armies or from entering into military
agreements on their own with other nations or
states.

ARTICLE II

Section 1

The executive Power shall be vested in a President of the United States of America. He shall hold his Office during the Term of four Years, and, together with the Vice President, chosen for the same Term, be elected, as follows:

★ The phrase "executive power," like the "necessary and proper" clause, is another of those terms in the Constitution that have led to endless debate as to just what it means. In Article II, which provides the basic design of the executive branch, the framers invest the president with this power, but never define it at anything like the length at which they set out the powers of Congress in Article I.

As for the president's term of office, at the Constitutional Convention there was considerable debate as to how long it should be. Most of the framers were anxious not to establish the kind of lifetime rule that a monarch ordinarily enjoys. But what would be too brief a term to ensure reasonable stability for the executive branch? Among the ideas put forward at the Convention were, at one end, a term of just two years, and at the other, an unlimited term during "good behavior"—which could have been used to justify a presidency of almost any length.

The delegates to the Convention knew that they were holding their debates in the presence of the man most likely to become the first president, George Washington, who had been elected unanimously as presiding officer of the Convention. Washington interpreted that position to mean he should take no part in the Convention's debates, so he was spared from having to express himself on the duration of the office he was likely to assume. During his presidency, Washington agonized frequently over how long he should serve. Though he would almost certainly have been elected to a third term, his decision to step down after two set a precedent that all of his successors observed until the 20th century, when Franklin D. Roosevelt ran successfully for the office four times. That led after Roosevelt's death to the adoption of the 22nd Amendment, which made a two-term limit a Constitutional requirement.

Each State shall appoint, in such Manner as the Legislature thereof may direct, a Number of Electors, equal to the whole Number of Senators and Representatives to which the State may be entitled in the Congress: but no Senator or Representative, or Person holding an Office of Trust or Profit under the United States, shall be appointed an Elector.

The Electors shall meet in their respective States, and vote by Ballot for two Persons, of whom one at least shall not be an Inhabitant of the same State with themselves. And they shall make a List of all the Persons voted for, and of the Number of Votes for each; which List they shall sign and certify, and transmit sealed to the Seat of the Government of the United States, directed to the President of the Senate. The President of the Senate shall, in the Presence of the Senate and House of Representatives, open all the Certificates, and the Votes shall then be counted. The Person having the greatest Number of Votes shall be the President, if such Number be a Majority of the whole Number of Electors appointed; and if there be more than one who have such Majority, and have an equal Number of Votes, then the House of Representatives shall immediately chuse by Ballot one of them for President; and if no Person have a Majority, then from the five highest on the List the said House shall in like Manner chuse the President. But in chusing the President, the Votes shall be taken by States, the Representation from each State having one Vote; a quorum for this Purpose shall consist of a Member or Members from two thirds of the States, and a Majority of all the States shall be necessary to a Choice. In every Case, after the Choice of the President, the Person having the greatest Number of Votes of the Electors shall be the Vice President. But if there should remain two or more who have equal Votes, the Senate shall chuse from them by Ballot the Vice President.

★ The electoral college, as we now call it, remains the most perplexing institution established by the Constitution. Strictly speaking, Americans do not elect their president. They choose "electors" on a statewide basis who then meet to choose the president. This convoluted arrangement was arrived at by the framers after lengthy debate over the question of how to select the chief executive. They worried that the American people could not be trusted to make an informed choice about a candidate for the highest national office. Under the system they designed, even Senators, a statewide office, were to be chosen by state legislatures.

For some time the framers considered having the president elected by Congress, but that would have violated the principle of separation of powers. The system they settled on instead provided that electors should meet in their separate states—not jointly in a single national gathering—to vote for two candidates. Their votes would be forwarded to Congress and tabulated by the president of the Senate. The candidate having the largest number—presuming that amounted to a majority of the votes—would become president; the runner up would be vice president. In the event of a tie, or a vote in which multiple candidates meant that none claimed a majority, the choice of president would be left to the House.

Early in the life of the new nation, that arrangement was thrown into crisis by the emergence of political parties, a development the framers did not foresee. They assumed that voters would choose electors as individuals, voting for them on the basis of individual merits and trusting them in turn to use their best judgment in selecting a president. But by the dawn of the 19th century parties had emerged—the Federalists, headed by then-President John Adams, and the Republicans, led by Thomas Jefferson. Electors ran together as a slate or "ticket," pledging in advance to vote for the candidates of their party. Voters chose electors in the expectation that they were in effect voting directly for their party's presidential and vice-presidential candidate.

In the election of 1800, however, Jefferson, whom the Republicans considered their presidential candidate, and Aaron Burr, whom they regarded as their vice-presidential candidate, both received the same number of electoral votes. That threw the contest into the outgoing House of Representatives, which was dominated by Federalists. This put the Federalists into the unusual position of deciding which member of the opposing party should be president. (Persuaded by the arch-Federalist Alexander Hamilton that Jefferson would be easier to work with, they chose him.) That tumultuous election led to changes in the system that were incorporated in the 12th Amendment in 1804, though even then the basic framework of what we now call the electoral college remained in place.

The Congress may determine the Time of chusing the Electors, and the Day on which they shall give their Votes; which Day shall be the same throughout the United States.

No Person except a natural born Citizen, or a Citizen of the United States, at the time of the Adoption of this Constitution, shall be eligible to the Office of President; neither shall any Person be eligible to that Office who shall not have attained to the Age of thirty five Years, and been fourteen Years a Resident within the United States.

★ The requirement that a president should be
a "natural born citizen" does not disqualify
candidates, like George Romney in 1968 and John
McCain in 2008, who were born abroad to parents
who were American citizens. For the nation's
highest office, the framers also set the highest
minimum age requirement—35 years.

In Case of the Removal of the President from Office, or of his Death,
Resignation, or Inability to discharge the Powers and Duties of
the said Office, the Same shall devolve on the Vice President, and
the Congress may by Law provide for the Case of Removal, Death,
Resignation or Inability, both of the President and Vice President,
declaring what Officer shall then act as President, and such Officer
shall act accordingly, until the Disability be removed, or a President
shall be elected.

★ Here the framers outline the vice president's most
fateful duty—to succeed a president who has
left office due to death, resignation or disability.
In the 25th Amendment, ratified in 1967, the
Constitution would clarify the means for declaring
a president too disabled to fulfill the duties of
office.

The President shall, at stated Times, receive for his Services, a Compensation, which shall neither be encreased nor diminished during
the Period for which he shall have been elected, and he shall not
receive within that Period any other Emolument from the United
States, or any of them.

★ This provision ensures that Congress cannot lower
the president's salary as a means to punish him
for opposing their will or raise it to reward him
for working with them. It also prevents individual
states from rewarding him financially for favoring
their interests.

Before he enter on the Execution of his Office, he shall take the following Oath or Affirmation:—"I do solemnly swear (or affirm) that I will faithfully execute the Office of President of the United States, and will to the best of my Ability, preserve, protect and defend the Constitution of the United States."

★ Historians disagree as to whether George Washington, when he first took the oath of office on April 30, 1789, spontaneously added the final words: "So help me, God," but those words have become a tradition.

Section 2

The President shall be Commander in Chief of the Army and Navy of the United States, and of the Militia of the several States, when called into the actual Service of the United States; he may require the Opinion, in writing, of the principal Officer in each of the executive Departments, upon any Subject relating to the Duties of their respective Offices, and he shall have Power to grant Reprieves and Pardons for Offences against the United States, except in Cases of Impeachment.

★ While Article I, Section 8 gives Congress the power "to declare war," here the framers make the president Commander in Chief, setting the stage for a multitude of conflicts between the two branches over their respective power to initiate and oversee military action.

The power to require written opinions from the heads of the various departments of the executive branch was included to emphasize that the president is truly head of the executive and not merely supervisor of semi-autonomous agencies.

After considering the possibility of conferring on the Senate the power to grant reprieves and pardons, the framers gave that ability exclusively to the president. Alexander Hamilton wrote in the Federalist 74, one of the essays in defense of the new Constitution that he produced after the Convention with James Madison and John Jay, "It is not to be doubted, that a single man of prudence and good sense is better fitted, in delicate conjunctures, to balance the motives which may plead for and against the remission of the punishment, than any numerous body whatever." After President Gerald Ford pardoned ex-President Richard Nixon in 1974, then-Senator Walter Mondale tried and failed to gain approval for an amendment that would give a two-third majority of Congress 180 days to nullify a presidential pardon it disapproved of. The idea was revived, and again failed, in 2001, shortly after President Bill Clinton's pardon of the fugitive financier Marc Rich.

He shall have Power, by and with the Advice and Consent of the Senate, to make Treaties, provided two thirds of the Senators present concur; and he shall nominate, and by and with the Advice and Consent of the Senate, shall appoint Ambassadors, other public Ministers and Consuls, Judges of the supreme Court, all other Officers of the United States, whose Appointments are not herein otherwise provided for, and which shall be established by Law: but the Congress may by Law vest the Appointment of such inferior Officers, as they think proper, in the President alone, in the Courts of Law, or in the Heads of Departments.

★ The "advice and consent" power of the Senate with respect to treaties is another that the framers left vague. Early in his Presidency, George Washington went to the Senate chamber to solicit members' views on a proposed treaty with several Native American tribes. He found the experience so inconclusive that he soon stopped seeking Senate advice in formulating the terms of any treaty still in negotiation. Thereafter he merely submitted treaties to the Senate to approve or

reject, but not to revise—a practice followed
by his successors. The "advice and consent"
power with respect to judges, ambassadors, and
other officers is one the Senate still exercises
aggressively, as the frequent Supreme Court
confirmation battles attest.

The President shall have Power to fill up all Vacancies that may
happen during the Recess of the Senate, by granting Commissions
which shall expire at the End of their next Session.

★ Presidents rely sometimes on this clause while
the Senate is in recess to appoint nominees who
have been refused Senate confirmation or are
likely to be refused—no matter that the vacancies
they were chosen to fill may have opened long
before the Senate went into recess.

Section 3

He shall from time to time give to the Congress Information
of the State of the Union, and recommend to their Consideration such Measures as he shall judge necessary and expedient;
he may, on extraordinary Occasions, convene both Houses, or
either of them, and in Case of Disagreement between them, with
Respect to the Time of Adjournment, he may adjourn them to such
Time as he shall think proper; he shall receive Ambassadors and
other public Ministers; he shall take Care that the Laws be faithfully executed, and shall Commission all the Officers of the United
States.

★ The obligation to give Congress "information of
the state of the union" provides the basis for
today's State of the Union address,
though the Constitution does not require it to
be delivered annually or even by way of a
speech. George Washington planted the seeds
of the modern tradition by doing both. But in

1801 President Thomas Jefferson, always on the lookout for any signs of "monarchical" pretensions in the presidency, decided that the annual address was one such sign and decided to send the information to Congress in writing. That continued to be the practice until 1913, when Woodrow Wilson revived the practice of annual remarks. Eleven years later Calvin Coolidge was the first president to broadcast his speech on radio. Even then, it wasn't known as the "State of the Union message," until Franklin D. Roosevelt called it that in 1935. In 1947 Harry Truman became the first president to deliver it on television.

Section 4

The President, Vice President and all civil Officers of the United States, shall be removed from Office on Impeachment for, and Conviction of, Treason, Bribery, or other high Crimes and Misdemeanors.

★ It was only late in the Constitutional Convention that the framers decided that the wide-ranging term "high crimes and misdemeanors" should be added to the more narrowly understood offenses of treason and bribery among the charges that could lead to impeachment. Two presidents have been impeached—Andrew Johnson in 1868 for actions to impede the policies of Reconstruction after the Civil War and Bill Clinton in 1999 for perjury and obstruction of justice in connection with his testimony about his relationship with a White House intern and the subsequent investigation into that testimony. Both men were acquitted by the Senate. In 1974 the House Judiciary Committee brought a bill of impeachment against Richard Nixon for his actions in connection with the Watergate break-in, but before the full House could approve it, which was considered a near-certainty, he resigned.

ARTICLE III

Section 1

The judicial Power of the United States shall be vested in one supreme Court, and in such inferior Courts as the Congress may from time to time ordain and establish. The Judges, both of the supreme and inferior Courts, shall hold their Offices during good Behaviour, and shall, at stated Times, receive for their Services a Compensation, which shall not be diminished during their Continuance in Office.

★ With this section the framers established the judicial branch, but as a start summoned up just one part, the Supreme Court, leaving it to Congress to decide whether there should be lower federal courts, and if so how many. This reflects a division at the Constitutional Convention. While the delegates largely agreed that the new nation needed a Supreme Court, especially to decide cases arising from disagreements between states, many felt that existing state courts were sufficient to enforce national laws. Congress would settle the matter in 1789, when it passed the first Judiciary Act, establishing a lower federal court system.

To help guarantee an independent judiciary, the framers also made it difficult to remove judges arbitrarily by declaring that they should hold office "during good behavior." (This was a standard established for the British judiciary in 1701. Before that, English judges served at the discretion of the Crown, a discretion frequently exercised.) To prevent judges from being penalized financially for their rulings, the framers also specified that their salaries cannot be reduced while they are on the court.

Section 2

The judicial Power shall extend to all Cases, in Law and Equity, arising under this Constitution, the Laws of the United States, and Treaties made, or which shall be made, under their Authority;—to all Cases affecting Ambassadors, other public Ministers and Consuls;—to all Cases of admiralty and maritime Jurisdiction;—to Controversies to which the United States shall be a Party;—to Controversies between two or more States;— between a State and Citizens of another State,—between Citizens of different States,—between Citizens of the same State claiming Lands under Grants of different States, and between a State, or the Citizens thereof, and foreign States, Citizens or Subjects.

★ By limiting the judicial power to "cases" and "controversies," the framers took a step to ensure that the Supreme Court should hear disputes only between real parties and not be enlisted by the president or Congress to serve as an advisor on legal questions that had not yet come before it.

By giving federal judges jurisdiction over all cases "in law and equity," the framers were providing them with powers that in England were divided between two systems—law courts and equity courts. Law courts, which relied upon the common law, tended to offer limited remedies, like financial compensation for an injury. But a person suing in equity court could seek a wider range of actions by the court, including injunctions intended to prohibit certain behavior before it occurred. The power to issue injunctions and pursue other broad remedies would be especially important in the Civil Rights era of the 1950s through the '70s, when courts were authorized to redraw school district lines or to order school busing to accomplish school integration.

Notably, the framers were silent on the question of whether the Supreme Court could exercise judicial

review—the power to declare federal or state laws
or actions by the other branches of the federal
government unconstitutional. That power has its
sources chiefly in the Supreme Court's 1803 ruling
in *Marbury* v. *Madison,* in which Chief Justice John
Marshall famously wrote that it is "emphatically
the province and duty of the judicial department to
say what the law is."

In all Cases affecting Ambassadors, other public Ministers and Consuls, and those in which a State shall be Party, the supreme Court shall have original Jurisdiction. In all the other Cases before mentioned, the supreme Court shall have appellate Jurisdiction, both as to Law and Fact, with such Exceptions, and under such Regulations as the Congress shall make.

The Trial of all Crimes, except in Cases of Impeachment, shall be by Jury; and such Trial shall be held in the State where the said Crimes shall have been committed; but when not committed within any State, the Trial shall be at such Place or Places as the Congress may by Law have directed.

Section 3

Treason against the United States, shall consist only in levying War against them, or in adhering to their Enemies, giving them Aid and Comfort. No Person shall be convicted of Treason unless on the Testimony of two Witnesses to the same overt Act, or on Confession in open Court.

★ Treason is the only crime that the Constitution
defines at length. It does that as a means to
prevent future governments from redefining it too
broadly, for instance to charge political offenders
as traitors.

The Congress shall have Power to declare the Punishment of Treason, but no Attainder of Treason shall work Corruption of Blood, or Forfeiture except during the Life of the Person attainted.

★ "No attainder of treason shall work corruption of blood." To modern ears this is the most archaic-sounding of any provision in the Constitution. But it sets out an important principle of a just society: That the penalties for treason, as determined by Congress, should only be applied to those convicted of that crime, not to their families.

ARTICLE IV

Section 1
Full Faith and Credit shall be given in each State to the public Acts, Records, and judicial Proceedings of every other State. And the Congress may by general Laws prescribe the Manner in which such Acts, Records and Proceedings shall be proved, and the Effect thereof.

★ As another means to unify the nation, this section requires every state to recognize as legitimate the laws and court judgments of all other states. But it also allows Congress to make laws determining the "effect" that a state law must have in other states. It was that language that opened the way for Congress in 1996 to pass the Defense of Marriage Act (DOMA), which allowed states that forbid marriage by same-sex couples to refuse to recognize such marriages performed in other states (in other words, to say they had "no effect").

The Citizens of each State shall be entitled to all Privileges and Immunities of Citizens in the several States.

★ Just as every state must recognize the laws of other states, each must grant to the citizens of other states the same legal rights and treatment under law that it gives its own citizens. Under the interpretation given to this provision by the Supreme Court, states must provide a significant justification for any measure discriminating against out-of-state residents. Over the years the court has struck down measures as diverse as discriminatory license fees for out-of-state shrimp catchers in South Carolina, a Georgia law that allowed only state residents to obtain abortions in Georgia, and an Alaska law that gave preference to Alaskans for jobs on the Alaska pipeline.

A Person charged in any State with Treason, Felony, or other Crime, who shall flee from Justice, and be found in another State, shall on Demand of the executive Authority of the State from which he fled, be delivered up, to be removed to the State having Jurisdiction of the Crime.

★ This section obliges states to honor requests from other states for the extradition of fugitives from justice.

No Person held to Service or Labour in one State, under the Laws thereof, escaping into another, shall, in Consequence of any Law or Regulation therein, be discharged from such Service or Labour, but shall be delivered up on Claim of the Party to whom such Service or Labour may be due.

★ Once again the framers avoid using the word "slaves" or "slavery." The purpose of this section is to address the problem of fugitive slaves and the responsibility of states, including states in which slavery was abolished, to assist in returning them to their "owners." In 1793 Congress passed the first fugitive-slave law, which laid out procedures for their return. But in the decades that followed, the issue of escaped slaves would become one of the most contentious in American law. Between 1842 and the start of the Civil War 19 years later, the Supreme Court would hear no fewer than four cases touching on the question. Ultimately it would be settled only by the outcome of the war and the 13th Amendment, which abolished slavery throughout the U.S.

Section 3

New States may be admitted by the Congress into this Union; but no new State shall be formed or erected within the Jurisdiction of any other State; nor any State be formed by the Junction of two or more States, or Parts of States, without the Consent of the Legislatures of the States concerned as well as of the Congress.

★ In 1787, the year of the Constitutional Convention, it was well understood that the vast territory between the seaboard states and the Mississippi River would eventually be divided into new states. With this provision the framers made clear that Congress could legitimately oversee the inevitable expansion of the U.S. They also prohibited the formation of new states within the territory of existing states unless the legislatures of both states and Congress approved. All the same, during the Civil War, West Virginia broke away from the slave state of Virginia after the latter seceded. Though Virginia did not consent, Congress granted West Virginia's application to join the Union.

The Congress shall have Power to dispose of and make all needful Rules and Regulations respecting the Territory or other Property belonging to the United States; and nothing in this Constitution shall be so construed as to Prejudice any Claims of the United States, or of any particular State.

★ Here the framers make fairly flexible rules for the power that Congress exercises—"to dispose of and make all needful rules and regulations"—over territories that have not yet become states. This too would become a vexing issue in the years leading up to the Civil War, when the nation became consumed by the question of whether to permit slavery on new territories. After the 1898 treaty that acknowledged the U.S. victory in the Spanish-American War, the Supreme Court would also have to deal repeatedly with the question of how the Constitution applied to territories, including Puerto Rico and the Philippines, that were ceded by Spain.

Section 4

The United States shall guarantee to every State in this Union a Republican Form of Government, and shall protect each of them against Invasion; and on Application of the Legislature, or of the Executive (when the Legislature cannot be convened), against domestic Violence.

★ The Constitution guarantees to every state "a republican form of government" but does not define it, though most of the framers would have agreed that the term described some form of representative government. The guarantee to states that they could count on the federal government to defend them against "domestic violence" was a response to Shays' Rebellion, the then-recent uprising of debt-ridden farmers and workers in western Massachusetts that the state had proven nearly incapable of suppressing.

ARTICLE V

The Congress, whenever two thirds of both Houses shall deem it necessary, shall propose Amendments to this Constitution, or, on the Application of the Legislatures of two thirds of the several States, shall call a Convention for proposing Amendments, which, in either Case, shall be valid to all Intents and Purposes, as Part of this Constitution, when ratified by the Legislatures of three fourths of the several States, or by Conventions in three fourths thereof, as the one or the other Mode of Ratification may be proposed by the Congress; Provided that no Amendment which may be made prior to the Year One thousand eight hundred and eight shall in any Manner affect the first and fourth Clauses in the Ninth Section of the first Article; and that no State, without its Consent, shall be deprived of its equal Suffrage in the Senate.

★ One of the objections to the Articles of Confederation had been that they could only be amended by the unanimous consent of all states, a barrier that proved impossible. The framers lowered the bar. Once an Amendment to the Constitution has been okayed by a two thirds majority of both houses of Congress, it needs to be approved only by three quarters of the states, either through their legislatures or through special state conventions. (The 21st Amendment, which repealed Prohibition in 1933, is so far the only one to have relied on the convention process.) The clause that specifies that before 1808 no amendment can interfere with portions of Article I, Section 9 was included to appease South Carolina and Georgia. It was designed to prevent changes that would penalize slavery or shut off the slave trade before that year. To satisfy the smaller states, the final clause guarantees that the Senate, where each state has two senators (no matter what its population), cannot be abolished by amendment.

ARTICLE VI

All Debts contracted and Engagements entered into, before the Adoption of this Constitution, shall be as valid against the United States under this Constitution, as under the Confederation.

★ One of the principal dilemmas of the new nation after the Revolutionary War was the question of how to repay the considerable wartime debt incurred by the individual states and the Continental Congress. This provision makes clear that the new government established by the Constitution could be counted on to honor those obligations. Devising a plan to consolidate and repay the debt would be one of the first priorities of Alexander Hamilton when he became treasury secretary under George Washington.

This Constitution, and the Laws of the United States which shall be made in Pursuance thereof; and all Treaties made, or which shall be made, under the Authority of the United States, shall be the supreme Law of the Land; and the Judges in every State shall be bound thereby, any Thing in the Constitution or Laws of any State to the Contrary notwithstanding.

★ At one point during the Constitutional Convention the framers considered a plan to give Congress the power to veto state laws. As an alternative they approved instead the federal "supremacy clause," which ensures that federal law takes precedence over state law in any situation where the two conflict and directs state judges to act accordingly.

The Senators and Representatives before mentioned, and the Members of the several State Legislatures, and all executive and judicial Officers, both of the United States and of the several States, shall be bound by Oath or Affirmation, to support this Constitution; but no religious Test shall ever be required as a Qualification to any Office or public Trust under the United States.

★ This provision marks the only place in the main text of the Constitution that refers to religion. In the 18th century religious tests were common in England, designed to exclude from office anyone—chiefly Roman Catholics and non-conforming Protestants—who was not a member of the Church of England. Some states, including Massachusetts and Pennsylvania, also had state constitutional provisions requiring of officials a belief in God or the Christian faith. The framers sought here to bar any such requirements for federal office holders.

ARTICLE VII
The Ratification of the Conventions of nine States, shall be sufficient for the Establishment of this Constitution between the States so ratifying the Same.

★ The Articles of Confederation could be amended only by the unanimous consent of all 13 states. But the framers had done more than amend the Articles; they had entirely discarded them. Requiring no more than nine states to ratify the Constitution made it far more likely that the new charter would go into effect. By putting the question of ratification before newly elected "conventions" the framers also sought to bypass state legislators who might be wary of any new government framework that could dilute their power. The conventions would also emphasize that the Constitution was a compact among the American people, not merely among the states.

The Signers

Done in Convention by the Unanimous Consent of the States present the Seventeenth Day of September in the Year of our Lord one thousand seven hundred and Eighty seven and of the Independance of the United States of America the Twelfth. In witness whereof We have hereunto subscribed our Names,

★ When the Constitutional Convention opened in the summer of 1787 there were 55 delegates gathered in the Pennsylvania State House. By the time the document was ready for signing, 41 remained. Only 38 of those present signed. (John Dickinson of Delaware, who had left a few days before the signing because of ill health, had his Delaware colleague George Read sign on his behalf, bringing the number of signatories to 39.) Three delegates declined to add their names owing to objections to various provisions. They were George Mason and Edmund Randolph of Virginia and Elbridge Gerry of Massachusetts.

ATTEST

William Jackson, Secretary

G°. Washington, President and deputy from Virginia

DELAWARE
Geo: Read
Gunning Bedford jun
John Dickinson
Richard Bassett
Jaco: Broom

MARYLAND
James McHenry
Dan of St Thos. Jenifer
Danl. Carroll

VIRGINIA
John Blair
James Madison Jr.

NORTH CAROLINA
Wm. Blount
Richd. Dobbs Spaight
Hu. Williamson

SOUTH CAROLINA
J. Rutledge
Charles Cotesworth Pinckney
Charles Pinckney
Pierce Butler

GEORGIA
William Few
Abr Baldwin

NEW HAMPSHIRE
John Langdon
Nicholas Gilman

MASSACHUSETTS
Nathaniel Gorham
Rufus King

CONNECTICUT
Wm. Saml. Johnson
Roger Sherman

NEW YORK
Alexander Hamilton

NEW JERSEY
Wil: Livingston
David Brearley
Wm. Paterson
Jona: Dayton

PENNSYLVANIA
B. Franklin
Thomas Mifflin
Robt. Morris
Geo. Clymer
Thos. FitzSimons
Jared Ingersoll
James Wilson
Gouv. Morris

The Amendments

Congress of the United States
begun and held at the
City of New-York, on
Wednesday the fourth of March,
one thousand seven hundred and eighty nine.

THE Conventions of a number of the States, having at the time of their adopting the Constitution, expressed a desire, in order to prevent misconstruction or abuse of its powers, that further declaratory and restrictive clauses should be added: And as extending the ground of public confidence in the Government, will best ensure the beneficent ends of its institution.

RESOLVED by the Senate and House of Representatives of the United States of America, in Congress assembled, two thirds of both Houses concurring, that the following Articles be proposed to the Legislatures of the several States, as amendments to the Constitution of the United States, all, or any of which Articles, when ratified by three fourths of the said Legislatures, to be valid to all intents and purposes, as part of the said Constitution; viz.

ARTICLES in addition to, and Amendment of the Constitution of the United States of America, proposed by Congress, and ratified by the Legislatures of the several States, pursuant to the fifth Article of the original Constitution.

★ The delegates to the Constitutional Convention considered including a Bill of Rights within their new document, but settled instead upon a promise to make that the first order of business for the new Congress they were establishing. To do otherwise would probably have meant additional months of wrangling in Philadelphia at a time when the framers were tired from their long efforts and ready to go home. As the preamble on the facing page notes, when the proposed Constitution was under consideration in the various state ratifying conventions, many there had also remarked on the importance of adding "further declaratory and restrictive clauses."

Accordingly, on June 8, 1789, James Madison introduced a series of 17 proposed amendments in the House of Representatives. Though he wanted them incorporated directly into the main text of the Constitution, he backed down in the face of arguments that Congress had no power to revise the language of the original document. On September 25, Congress approved and transmitted to the states a package of just 12 amendments. By December 15, 1791, ten of those had been approved by the necessary three-fourths majority of the states. To this day we call those first ten amendments, as Madison did, the Bill of Rights.

AMENDMENT I

Congress shall make no law respecting an establishment of religion, or prohibiting the free exercise thereof; or abridging the freedom of speech, or of the press; or the right of the people peaceably to assemble, and to petition the Government for a redress of grievances.

★ Touching upon core values of a free society—freedom of religion, speech, the press, and assembly—the remarkably compact First Amendment has long been one of the most powerful and hotly contested provisions of the Constitution. The language forbidding the government to favor any religion originally constrained actions only by the federal government. In the 19th century, for instance, many states continued to provide public support to favored denominations. It was only in the 20th century that this changed, due to the court doctrine called "incorporation." Armed with the language of the 14th Amendment forbidding states to "abridge the privileges and immunities" of U.S. citizens or deny them "equal protection of the laws," courts increasingly held that the Bill of Rights applied to actions by state governments as well as to the federal government and obliged them to recognize the constitutional rights of their citizens. But disputes continue to arise over questions such as whether governments can offer aid to parochial schools or permit religious symbols on public property.

Remarkably, in light of its importance to us today and the many Supreme Court decisions it has given rise to, the Supreme Court's first major rulings on the free speech provision of the First Amendment did not begin until after World I. In particular, in 1919 Justice Oliver Wendell Holmes, in *Schenck* v. *United States,* articulated his famous "clear and present danger" standard for determining what kinds of speech government might legitimately limit, offering his now famous example of a man falsely shouting "fire" in a crowded theater. Yet in that ruling Holmes and the Court actually upheld the conviction of a man sentenced for distributing 15,000 leaflets arguing that people should peacefully resist the World War I draft law. But within the year Holmes would dissent, in *Abrams* v. *United States,* from a court ruling that upheld another set of convictions, this time of five Russian immigrants who had called for a general strike to protest the decision of President Woodrow Wilson to send American troops to Russia. In that dissent Holmes argued for the importance of the "free trade in ideas," writing that "the best test of truth is the power of the thought to get itself accepted in the competition of the market."

AMENDMENT II

A well regulated Militia, being necessary to the security of a free State, the right of the people to keep and bear Arms, shall not be infringed.

★ To early Americans, state militias represented a line of defense against the possibility that a standing national army could be used to suppress the rights of citizens and states. In the modern controversy over gun control, the Second Amendment has led to endless arguments over whether it was fashioned to guarantee an individual right to firearms, or merely to safeguard the right to keep and bear them as part of a "well regulated militia." Before the 20th century the Supreme Court heard few Second Amendment cases, in part because there were few laws regulating firearms outside the South, where laws often barred African-Americans from owning them.

With the rise of organized crime during Prohibition, Congress passed the National Firearms Act of 1934, which required owners to register sawed off shotguns and automatic weapons and imposed taxes on them. In the 1939 ruling *United States* v. *Miller* the Court held that because such weapons were not part of the equipment of an ordinary militia they were not protected by the Second Amendment. But in its 2008 ruling, *District of Columbia* v. *Heller,* which overturned a handgun ban in the U.S. capital, the Court changed direction, recognizing an individual right to bear arms while also allowing that government can regulate firearms in some circumstances.

Amendment III

No Soldier shall, in time of peace be quartered in any house, without the consent of the Owner, nor in time of war, but in a manner to be prescribed by law.

★ This amendment forbids a practice that's virtually unknown today, but was still a sore point in late 18th century America. During the Revolutionary War British soldiers were sometimes assigned to "quarters" in American homes, often with unwilling hosts. This amendment forbids the practice for American soldiers entirely in time of peace, and allows it in wartime only under such circumstances as the law permits. In more recent years the Third Amendment has also provided one support for the idea that the Constitution contains an implicit "right of privacy," which the Court has used to uphold laws legalizing birth control and abortion.

AMENDMENT IV

The right of the people to be secure in their persons, houses, papers, and effects, against unreasonable searches and seizures, shall not be violated, and no Warrants shall issue, but upon probable cause, supported by Oath or affirmation, and particularly describing the place to be searched, and the persons or things to be seized.

★ This is another provision that grew out of American experience under British rule, when British soldiers, custom agents and other authorities frequently used open-ended general warrants, often based on no firm suspicions—no "probable cause"—to conduct blanket searches without a magistrate's authorization. The Fourth Amendment now stands as a foundation of the right to put limits on the power of police and other authorities, including public schools and public employers, to conduct wiretaps and other electronic surveillance or procedures like sobriety and drug tests. In the important 1961 ruling *Mapp* v. *Ohio* the Supreme Court ruled that courts could exclude trial evidence that police had obtained by improper means.

AMENDMENT V

No person shall be held to answer for a capital, or otherwise infamous crime, unless on a presentment or indictment of a Grand Jury, except in cases arising in the land or naval forces, or in the Militia, when in actual service in time of War or public danger; nor shall any person be subject for the same offence to be twice put in jeopardy of life or limb; nor shall be compelled in any criminal case to be a witness against himself, nor be deprived of life, liberty, or property, without due process of law; nor shall private property be taken for public use, without just compensation.

★ The first part of the Fifth Amendment ensures that citizens, or at least civilians, who are accused of a serious federal crime must be brought before a grand jury of ordinary citizens, whose job it is to determine if the government has sufficient evidence to bring the charge. (Many states still do not require grand jury indictments for serious state crimes.) The prohibition against "double jeopardy," or being tried twice or more for the same crime, enshrines in the Constitution a longtime principle of English common law. So does the ban on self-incrimination, a protection that has become famous to Americans as "taking the Fifth." It also serves as the basis for parts of the Supreme Court's 1966 ruling in *Miranda* v. *Arizona* that persons in custody must be informed by police that they have the right to remain silent and that anything they say may be used against them in court. The amendment then promises that no one can be deprived of "life, liberty or property" without "due process of law," a broad phrase meant to curtail the abuse of power by government. The last portion, the so-called "takings clause," is designed to ensure that government cannot simply seize private property— for instance, to build highways or airports under its power of "eminent domain"—without paying for it.

Amendment VI

In all criminal prosecutions, the accused shall enjoy the right to a speedy and public trial, by an impartial jury of the State and district wherein the crime shall have been committed, which district shall have been previously ascertained by law, and to be informed of the nature and cause of the accusation; to be confronted with the witnesses against him; to have compulsory process for obtaining witnesses in his favor, and to have the Assistance of Counsel for his defence.

★ The right to a speedy and public trial ensures that government ordinarily cannot hold accused persons for long periods, a form of punishment in itself. Neither can it conduct secret trials along the line of the English Court of Star Chamber, which was abolished in the 17th century but long remained a symbol of despotic procedure. The guarantee that jury trials must take place in the "district" where the crime occurred prevents government from assigning the accused to trial in distant locations. Courts have been permitted, however, to move highly publicized trials when it appeared that pre-trial publicity might make it impossible to find an impartial local jury.

The Supreme Court has held that the right "to be informed of the nature and cause of the accusation" forbids charges formulated in language that is too general or far reaching. The clause concerning witnesses ensures, among other things, that the accused may cross-examine witnesses against him and use subpoena power to require witnesses to appear in court. Finally, the stipulation that the accused has the right of counsel serves as the basis for the second portion of the "Miranda warning." Growing out of the court's 1966 ruling in *Miranda* v. *Arizona,* this requires police to inform the accused that he or she has the right to an attorney and to have that attorney present during police questioning. It also requires that if they cannot afford one a court-appointed attorney will be provided at no cost. The right to a court-appointed attorney in all felony cases had been given its definitive statement by the court just three years earlier, in its landmark 1963 ruling in *Gideon* v. *Wainwright.*

AMENDMENT VII

In Suits at common law, where the value in controversy shall exceed twenty dollars, the right of trial by jury shall be preserved, and no fact tried by a jury, shall be otherwise re-examined in any Court of the United States, than according to the rules of the common law.

★ This amendment strikes modern ears as somewhat peculiar—"twenty dollars"?—but in its first part it was meant to ensure that jury trials would be used in civil suits as well as in criminal cases, something that opponents of the Constitution felt was not guaranteed in the original document. The second part, restricting judges from re-examining the facts determined by a jury except by the rules of common law, put limits on the power of federal judges to set aside jury verdicts.

AMENDMENT VIII

Excessive bail shall not be required, nor excessive fines imposed, nor cruel and unusual punishments inflicted.

★ The Eighth Amendment does not attempt to quantify "excessive" bails or fines—no "twenty-dollar" rule here—but it lays down a reminder that accused persons are innocent until proven guilty and should not be burdened with bail that is impossible to meet, which might require them to languish in prison unnecessarily before they stand trial. Neither should those who have been convicted be subject to monetary penalties out of proportion to their crimes.

The prohibition against "cruel and unusual punishment" has set the stage for the modern debate over the death penalty, which was widely accepted in 18th century America. Death penalty opponents argue that the notion of cruel and unusual is an evolving standard. But except for a few years in the 1970s, the Supreme Court has held that the Amendment does not prohibit capital punishment.

AMENDMENT IX

The enumeration in the Constitution, of certain rights, shall not be construed to deny or disparage others retained by the people.

★ This is a provision of the Constitution that the courts rarely address, but it was important to early Americans, who feared that if they produced a Constitution that enumerated many specific rights, it might be assumed that any they failed to mention were rights they did not intend to secure. The Ninth Amendment is a broad assertion that rights not named in the text might still be retained by the people.

AMENDMENT X

The powers not delegated to the United States by the Constitution, nor prohibited by it to the States, are reserved to the States respectively, or to the people.

★ When the 1787 text of the Constitution was sent out to state ratifying conventions, this was one of the guarantees that "antifederalists"— those who were suspicious of a stronger central government—were most anxious to add to the document. When James Madison unveiled it as part of his proposed amendments in the first Congress, some members sought to strengthen the amendment by changing its terms to read "powers not expressly delegated" to the U.S.—a proposal the House voted down 32–17. Though there have been periods, especially in the late 19th and early 20th century, when the Supreme Court has relied on the Tenth Amendment to strike down federal laws, overall the Amendment has not become an instrument for opposing federal power. But it remains a perennial arguing point for advocates of states' rights.

AMENDMENT XI

Passed by Congress: March 4, 1794
Ratified: February 7, 1795

The Judicial power of the United States shall not be construed to extend to any suit in law or equity, commenced or prosecuted against one of the United States by Citizens of another State, or by Citizens or Subjects of any Foreign State.

★ This amendment, the first to be ratified after the Bill of Rights four years earlier, is one of only two adopted expressly to counteract a decision of the Supreme Court. (The other is the 16th, which gave Congress the power to tax individual incomes directly.) It modifies the portion of Article III, Section 2 that specified the kind of cases that the newly created federal courts could hear. Among those were disputes between "a State and Citizens of another State." Accordingly, in 1793 the Supreme Court ruled in *Chisolm* v. *Georgia* that it could hear a case brought against the state of Georgia by a citizen of South Carolina (who was the executor of an estate seeking payment for supplies provided to Georgia during the Revolutionary War). The English common principle of "sovereign immunity" had long held that a government cannot be sued without its consent. But when Georgia refused to appear in court, the justices ruled 4–1 in favor of the plaintiff. The decision caused such an uproar that the 11th Amendment, which stripped the court of that power, was quickly drafted and approved.

AMENDMENT XII

Passed by Congress: December 9, 1803
Ratified: June 15, 1804

The Electors shall meet in their respective states and vote by ballot for President and Vice-President, one of whom, at least, shall not be an inhabitant of the same state with themselves; they shall name in their ballots the person voted for as President, and in distinct ballots the person voted for as Vice-President, and they shall make distinct lists of all persons voted for as President, and of all persons voted for as Vice-President, and of the number of votes for each, which lists they shall sign and certify, and transmit sealed to the seat of the government of the United States, directed to the President of the Senate;—the President of the Senate shall, in the presence of the Senate and House of Representatives, open all the certificates and the votes shall then be counted;—The person having the greatest number of votes for President, shall be the President, if such number be a majority of the whole number of Electors appointed; and if no person have such majority, then from the persons having the highest numbers not exceeding three on the list of those voted for as President, the House of Representatives shall choose immediately, by ballot, the President. But in choosing the President, the votes shall be taken by states, the representation from each state having one vote; a quorum for this purpose shall consist of a member or members from two-thirds of the states, and a majority of all the states shall be necessary to a choice. And if the House of Representatives shall not choose a President whenever the right of choice shall devolve upon them, before the fourth day of March next following, then the Vice-President shall act as President, as in case of the death or other constitutional disability of the President. The person having the greatest number of votes as Vice-President, shall be the Vice-President, if such number be a majority of the whole number of Electors appointed, and if no person have a majority, then from the two highest numbers on the list, the Senate shall choose the Vice-President; a quorum for the purpose shall consist of two-thirds of the whole number of Senators, and a majority of the whole number shall be necessary to a choice. But no person constitutionally ineligible to the office of President shall be eligible to that of Vice-President of the United States.

★ This amendment modifies Article II, Section 1 of the Constitution, which established the complicated system of electors for the president and vice president. The framers expected voters to choose electors as individuals, who would likewise cast their votes for president on the basis of a candidate's individual merits. The electors were also expected to cast two ballots. The candidate receiving the largest number would become president; the runner-up, vice president. But with the rise of political parties electors were pledged in advance to vote for the "tickets" of their parties. And in the election of 1800, Thomas Jefferson and Aaron Burr, both representing the Republican party, received an equal number of votes, though it had been the party's intention that Jefferson should become president and Burr the vice president. The election was sent to the House, where Jefferson finally prevailed. The 12th Amendment required that, in future, electors would vote separately for the two offices. It also reduced from five to three the number of candidates the House would choose among in the event that no candidate received a majority of electoral votes.

AMENDMENT XIII
Passed by Congress: January 31, 1865
Ratified: December 6, 1865

Section 1
Neither slavery nor involuntary servitude, except as a punishment for crime whereof the party shall have been duly convicted, shall exist within the United States, or any place subject to their jurisdiction.

Section 2
Congress shall have power to enforce this article by appropriate legislation.

★ It took the Civil War to resolve at last the conflict over slavery that the framers had labored to avoid addressing directly. The 13th Amendment was the first of three far-reaching additions to the Constitution ratified in the years just after the war. Section 2, which explicitly empowers Congress to adopt any necessary further measures to enforce the amendment, was added in part because the Supreme Court, which had upheld slavery in the infamous Dred Scott ruling of 1857—a decision this amendment effectively overturned—was not trusted to do the job. Congress soon approved the Civil Rights Act of 1866 to overrule so-called "Black Codes" adopted by former states of the Confederacy to deny or curtail the right of newly freed slaves to own property, testify in court against whites, enter into contracts, travel, speak in public, assemble, or bear arms. The Black Codes would be short-lived, but they would provide a basis for Jim Crow laws that would later proliferate across the South to accomplish the same denial of basic rights to African-Americans. It would require the Civil Rights revolution of the 1960s to more completely follow through on the process of full citizenship that abolition merely set in motion.

AMENDMENT XIV
Passed by Congress: June 13, 1866
Ratified: July 9, 1868

Section 1
All persons born or naturalized in the United States, and subject to the jurisdiction thereof, are citizens of the United States and of the State wherein they reside. No State shall make or enforce any law which shall abridge the privileges or immunities of citizens of the United States; nor shall any State deprive any person of life, liberty, or property, without due process of law; nor deny to any person within its jurisdiction the equal protection of the laws.

Section 2
Representatives shall be apportioned among the several States according to their respective numbers, counting the whole number of persons in each State, excluding Indians not taxed. But when the right to vote at any election for the choice of electors for President and Vice-President of the United States, Representatives in Congress, the Executive and Judicial officers of a State, or the members of the Legislature thereof, is denied to any of the male inhabitants of such State, being twenty-one years of age, and citizens of the United States, or in any way abridged, except for participation in rebellion, or other crime, the basis of representation therein shall be reduced in the proportion which the number of such male citizens shall bear to the whole number of male citizens twenty-one years of age in such State.

Section 3
No person shall be a Senator or Representative in Congress, or elector of President and Vice-President, or hold any office, civil or

military, under the United States, or under any State, who, having previously taken an oath, as a member of Congress, or as an officer of the United States, or as a member of any State legislature, or as an executive or judicial officer of any State, to support the Constitution of the United States, shall have engaged in insurrection or rebellion against the same, or given aid or comfort to the enemies thereof. But Congress may by a vote of two-thirds of each House, remove such disability.

Section 4
The validity of the public debt of the United States, authorized by law, including debts incurred for payment of pensions and boun-ties for services in suppressing insurrection or rebellion, shall not be questioned. But neither the United States nor any State shall as-sume or pay any debt or obligation incurred in aid of insurrection or rebellion against the United States, or any claim for the loss or emancipation of any slave; but all such debts, obligations and claims shall be held illegal and void.

Section 5
The Congress shall have the power to enforce, by appropriate legislation, the provisions of this article.

★ No addition to the Constitution has proven to be more powerful or far reaching than the 14th Amendment. None has done more to create a nation in which the federal government has the power to remedy injustices done to citizens by the action of states. Section 1, with its guarantee of "equal protection of the law" and "due process" and its directive that no law should abridge the "privileges and immunities of citizens," ensured that Congress would have clear Constitutional support for its actions under the Civil Rights Act of 1866.

Section 2 was drafted to ensure the vote to freed slaves. It effectively repeals the provision of the Constitution that allowed slave states to count slaves as three-fifths of a person for purposes of deciding their population and thus how many Representatives each state could send to Congress. It also stipulates that any state that withholds the vote from its citizens—or at least its males over the age of 21—will have its citizen head count reduced in proportion to the number it disenfranchises. (Despite the new amendment, in the 1870s, as whites regained control of Southern legislatures, they were able to deny voting rights to African-Americans without interference from Congress.) Section 2 does however allow states to deny the right to vote to former Confederates, for "participation in rebellion."

Section 3 prohibits former Confederates from becoming office holders, as many attempted to do right after the Civil War, until such time as Congress should decide to lift that ban.

With the Civil War debt in mind, Section 4 guarantees that the federal debt will be honored, while at the same time forbidding government responsibility for Confederate debt. It also made clear that former slave owners would not be compensated for the "lost" economic value of their freed slaves.

The possibilities inherent in the 14th Amendment would not be fully explored until the 20th century. For decades after it was ratified, the Supreme Court would give a narrow interpretation of its guarantees. In particular, it did not hold that the Amendment required state and local government to adhere to the Bill of Rights. In one of the most notable examples, in 1896 the Court ruled in *Plessy* v. *Ferguson* that a Louisiana law requiring racial segregation of railway cars did not violate the equal protection clause.

In the early 20th century, however, the Court began
to apply the Bill of Rights to states more frequently,
especially after *Gitlow* v. *New York*, a 1925 ruling that
the First Amendment protections of free speech and
the press applied to the states. After World War II the
Court also made frequent use of the equal-protection
clause to block discriminatory state action, especially
on the basis of race or gender. Among the rulings that
relied on that clause was *Brown* v. *Board of Education*
(1954), which declared segregated schools to be
unconstitutional.

AMENDMENT XV

Passed by Congress: February 26, 1869
Ratified: February 3, 1870

Section 1
The right of citizens of the United States to vote shall not be denied
or abridged by the United States or by any State on account of race,
color, or previous condition of servitude.

Section 2
The Congress shall have the power to enforce this article by appropriate legislation.

★ Whereas the 14th Amendment specified
penalties for states that denied the vote to any
of its male citizens 21 years of age and above,
this Amendment puts the voting rights of freed
slaves explicitly into the Constitution. Even so,
Southern states would increasingly find ways
to disenfranchise black citizens through such
measures as literacy tests and poll taxes,
supported when necessary by outright intimidation
and violence. It would take the Voting Rights Act
of 1965 to fully ensure that the right to vote would
not be abridged for reasons of race or color.

AMENDMENT XVI
Passed by Congress: July 2, 1909
Ratified: February 3, 1913

The Congress shall have power to lay and collect taxes on incomes, from whatever source derived, without apportionment among the several States, and without regard to any census or enumeration.

★ Throughout the 19th century the question of whether Congress had the power to tax individual incomes led to controversy. The chief issue revolved around whether an income tax was a "direct tax." If so, it was unconstitutional, since the Constitution stipulated that direct taxes could only be levied by Congress on the states in proportion to their respective populations. All the same, a temporary income tax imposed during the Civil War was upheld by the Supreme Court in 1881 as an indirect tax. But in a highly charged 1895 case, *Pollock v. Farmers' Loan & Trust Co.*, the Court struck down a peacetime income tax law passed the previous year, a "flat tax" of 2% on all incomes above $4,000. This amendment overturned most of that ruling. In October, 1913, just eight months after the amendment was ratified, Congress passed a federal income tax law, this time with a graduated rate that imposed higher tax rates on higher incomes.

AMENDMENT XVII

Passed by Congress: May 13, 1912
Ratified: April 8, 1913

The Senate of the United States shall be composed of two Senators from each State, elected by the people thereof, for six years; and each Senator shall have one vote. The electors in each State shall have the qualifications requisite for electors of the most numerous branch of the State legislatures.

When vacancies happen in the representation of any State in the Senate, the executive authority of such State shall issue writs of election to fill such vacancies: Provided, That the legislature of any State may empower the executive thereof to make temporary appointments until the people fill the vacancies by election as the legislature may direct.

This amendment shall not be so construed as to affect the election or term of any Senator chosen before it becomes valid as part of the Constitution.

★ Article I, Section 3 mandates that Senators be elected not by the voters but by state legislatures. By this, the framers hoped to insulate the Senate, as the "upper chamber" of Congress, from popular passions. But by the late 19th century, direct election of Senators had become a rallying cry of the Progressives, who saw the Senate as a hotbed of wealth and privilege whose members were often chosen by corrupt means. This amendment ensured that the Senate, like the House, would be chosen by voters.

Amendment XVIII
Passed by Congress: December 18, 1917
Ratified: January 16, 1919

Section 1
After one year from the ratification of this article the manufacture, sale, or transportation of intoxicating liquors within, the importation thereof into, or the exportation thereof from the United States and all territory subject to the jurisdiction thereof for beverage purposes is hereby prohibited.

Section 2
The Congress and the several States shall have concurrent power to enforce this article by appropriate legislation.

Section 3
This article shall be inoperative unless it shall have been ratified as an amendment to the Constitution by the legislatures of the several States, as provided in the Constitution, within seven years from the date of the submission hereof to the States by the Congress.

★ The amendment that prohibited the "manufacture, sale, or transportation of intoxicating liquor" was the only one designed to limit rather than protect the rights of Americans and the only one to be repealed by a later amendment. It was the fruit of the temperance movement, a decades-long crusade against alcohol. In the 1850s a dozen states, starting with Maine, enacted bans on alcohol. By the end of that decade all of them had repealed the laws in the face of citizen opposition, but after the Civil War, a number of states and localities once again adopted similar bans. Temperance activists pushed for a nationwide ban, despite the unpopularity of the idea in cities, especially those where immigrants had brought from Europe a culture of wine and beer. Section 3 of the 18th Amendment, requiring that the ratification process be completed within seven years, was added by the Senate in the hope that the anti-alcohol forces could be held off for that long. It was the first instance of a time limit provision being included in the text of an amendment, a practice that would later become common. But it failed in its purpose. Within 13 months, 44 state legislatures had voted to ratify. Soon after, Congress adopted the Volstead Act, the law that created the framework for implementing Prohibition.

AMENDMENT XIX

Passed by Congress: June 4, 1919
Ratified: August 18, 1920

The right of citizens of the United States to vote shall not be denied or abridged by the United States or by any State on account of sex.

Congress shall have power to enforce this article by appropriate legislation.

★ An amendment to give the vote to women was first introduced in Congress in 1878. A decade later came another written in substantially the same language that the 19th Amendment would eventually use. When supporters of women's suffrage failed to get their amendment through Congress, they turned to state legislatures. By 1912 nine Western states had granted women the vote. Suffragists also resorted at times to the courts, but with less success. In particular, in 1875 the Supreme Court rejected the argument that a woman's right to vote was guaranteed under the "privileges and immunities" clause of the 14th Amendment. By the time the 19th Amendment was ratified, Congress already included its first woman, Rep. Jeanette Rankin of Montana, first elected in 1917.

AMENDMENT XX
Passed by Congress: March 2, 1932
Ratified: January 23, 1933

Section 1
The terms of the President and the Vice President shall end at noon on the 20th day of January, and the terms of Senators and Representatives at noon on the 3d day of January, of the years in which such terms would have ended if this article had not been ratified; and the terms of their successors shall then begin.

Section 2
The Congress shall assemble at least once in every year, and such meeting shall begin at noon on the 3d day of January, unless they shall by law appoint a different day.

Section 3
If, at the time fixed for the beginning of the term of the President, the President elect shall have died, the Vice President elect shall become President. If a President shall not have been chosen before the time fixed for the beginning of his term, or if the President elect shall have failed to qualify, then the Vice President elect shall act as President until a President shall have qualified; and the Congress may by law provide for the case wherein neither a President elect nor a Vice President shall have qualified, declaring who shall then act as President, or the manner in which one who is to act shall be selected, and such person shall act accordingly until a President or Vice President shall have qualified.

Section 4

The Congress may by law provide for the case of the death of any of the persons from whom the House of Representatives may choose a President whenever the right of choice shall have devolved upon them, and for the case of the death of any of the persons from whom the Senate may choose a Vice President whenever the right of choice shall have devolved upon them.

Section 5

Sections 1 and 2 shall take effect on the 15th day of October following the ratification of this article.

Section 6

This article shall be inoperative unless it shall have been ratified as an amendment to the Constitution by the legislatures of three-fourths of the several States within seven years from the date of its submission.

★ This amendment eliminated the unproductive "lame duck" sessions of Congress during even numbered years that had been created by Article I, Section 4 of the Constitution. It also partly remedied the problem of lame-duck presidencies by moving up the date of the presidential inauguration from March to January, shortening the time that a president who had not been re-elected remained in office before his successor assumed the presidency. Finally it clarified some problems of presidential succession—for instance, that the vice-president elect would become president-elect in the event that the president-elect should die before taking office.

Amendment XXI

Passed by Congress: February 20, 1933
Ratified: December 5, 1933

Section 1

The eighteenth article of amendment to the Constitution of the United States is hereby repealed.

Section 2

The transportation or importation into any State, Territory, or Possession of the United States for delivery or use therein of intoxicating liquors, in violation of the laws thereof, is hereby prohibited.

Section 3

This article shall be inoperative unless it shall have been ratified as an amendment to the Constitution by conventions in the several States, as provided in the Constitution, within seven years from the date of the submission hereof to the States by the Congress.

★ Prohibition proved to be a massive failure. Though it sharply curtailed alcohol consumption in the U.S., it never ended it. (And the consumption of alcohol was actually not the thing the 18th Amendment prohibited—merely its manufacture, sale, and transportation.) Federal, state, and local law enforcement was overwhelmed by the effort to enforce the ban. Worse, organized crime on a scale unknown in the U.S. emerged to provide the forbidden liquor citizens wanted. The 21st Amendment did not explicitly restore the right to produce and sell alcohol but it returned to states the right to regulate it as they saw fit. To establish a means for direct expression of popular approval for the amendment, and to fend off opposition to repeal in state legislatures where temperance forces still had influence, Section 3 places ratification in the hands of state conventions. It also put a seven-year time limit on the process. In fact, it took just a little over nine months from the time Congress approved the amendment until a sufficient number of state conventions had ratified it.

AMENDMENT XXII

Adopted by Congress: March 21, 1947
Ratified: February 27, 1951

Section 1

No person shall be elected to the office of the President more than twice, and no person who has held the office of President, or acted as President, for more than two years of a term to which some other person was elected President shall be elected to the office of President more than once. But this Article shall not apply to any person holding the office of President when this Article was proposed by Congress, and shall not prevent any person who may be holding the office of President, or acting as President, during the term within which this Article becomes operative from holding the office of President or acting as President during the remainder of such term.

Section 2

This article shall be inoperative unless it shall have been ratified as an amendment to the Constitution by the legislatures of three-fourths of the several States within seven years from the date of its submission to the States by the Congress.

★ George Washington's decision to step down from the presidency at the end of his second term became a precedent that was followed by all of his successors until Franklin Delano Roosevelt. Running as a wartime leader, Roosevelt was easily re-elected to a third and then a fourth term. But after his death in April 1945 the Republicans who soon after took control of Congress pushed to make the two-term limit a constitutional requirement.

AMENDMENT XXIII

Adopted by Congress: June 16, 1960
Ratified: March 29, 1961

Section 1

The District constituting the seat of Government of the United States shall appoint in such manner as Congress may direct: A number of electors of President and Vice President equal to the whole number of Senators and Representatives in Congress to which the District would be entitled if it were a State, but in no event more than the least populous State; they shall be in addition to those appointed by the States, but they shall be considered, for the purposes of the election of President and Vice President, to be electors appointed by a State; and they shall meet in the District and perform such duties as provided by the twelfth article of amendment.

Section 2

The Congress shall have power to enforce this article by appropriate legislation.

★ The Constitution provided representation for the citizens of "states." It also gave Congress the power to establish for the nation's capital a "federal district" outside the territory of any state. And so for almost two centuries citizens of the District of Columbia, established on land ceded by Maryland and Virginia, existed in a sort of legal limbo with respect to the democratic process at the federal level. This amendment extended to them for the first time the right to vote in presidential elections. Or, to put it in the language of the electoral college "to choose electors" equal to the number of Senators and House members the District would have if it were a state—though no more than the number of electors of the least populous state, which is presently three. The version of this amendment approved by the Senate would also have given the District a Representative in Congress, but the House revised it to produce the current, more limited language. For now the nation's capital sends a Representative who can speak from the House floor but cannot vote on the final passage of legislation.

AMENDMENT XXIV

Adopted by Congress: August 27, 1962
Ratified: January 23, 1964

Section 1

The right of citizens of the United States to vote in any primary or other election for President or Vice President, for electors for President or Vice President, or for Senator or Representative in Congress, shall not be denied or abridged by the United States or any State by reason of failure to pay poll tax or other tax.

Section 2

The Congress shall have power to enforce this article by appropriate legislation.

★ The poll tax—a levy imposed on voters—was a means by which Southern states attempted to keep African-Americans from voting. By 1964 only five states still required it, but it remained a hated symbol of obstacles put in the way of full citizenship for black Americans. Even after the amendment was ratified, some Southern states attempted to retain the tax for state elections. In 1966 the Supreme Court struck down those laws as a violation of the equal-protection clause of the 14th Amendment.

AMENDMENT XXV
Adopted by Congress: July 6, 1965
Ratified: February 10, 1967

Section 1
In case of the removal of the President from office or of his death or resignation, the Vice President shall become President.

Section 2
Whenever there is a vacancy in the office of the Vice President, the President shall nominate a Vice President who shall take office upon confirmation by a majority vote of both Houses of Congress.

Section 3
Whenever the President transmits to the President pro tempore of the Senate and the Speaker of the House of Representatives his written declaration that he is unable to discharge the powers and duties of his office, and until he transmits to them a written declaration to the contrary, such powers and duties shall be discharged by the Vice President as Acting President.

Section 4
Whenever the Vice President and a majority of either the principal officers of the executive departments or of such other body as Congress may by law provide, transmit to the President pro tempore of the Senate and the Speaker of the House of Representatives their written declaration that the President is unable to discharge the powers and duties of his office, the Vice President shall immediately assume the powers and duties of the office as Acting President.

Thereafter, when the President transmits to the President pro tempore of the Senate and the Speaker of the House of Representatives his written declaration that no inability exists, he shall resume the powers and duties of his office unless the Vice President and a majority of either the principal officers of the executive department or of such other body as Congress may by law provide, transmit within four days to the President pro tempore of the Senate and the Speaker of the House of Representatives their written declaration that the President is unable to discharge the powers and duties of his office. Thereupon Congress shall decide the issue, assembling within forty-eight hours for that purpose if not in session. If the Congress, within twenty-one days after receipt of the latter written declaration, or, if Congress is not in session, within twenty-one days after Congress is required to assemble, determines by two-thirds vote of both houses that the President is unable to discharge the powers and duties of his office, the Vice President shall continue to discharge the same as Acting President; otherwise, the President shall resume the powers and duties of his office.

★ This amendment was designed to clarify the situation when a president dies in office or is disabled. Article II, Section 1 of the Constitution provided that the vice president shall "discharge the Powers and Duties" of the president in the event of the latter's "Death, Resignation, or Inability." This amendment made clear that the vice president actually becomes president in the event of his predecessor's death and does not merely carry out, or "discharge," his duties. Article II also did not establish procedures to determine that a living president was disabled, as well as to allow him to resume office should he recover. After President James Garfield was shot by an assassin in 1881, he lay in a coma for two months before his death. In 1919 President Woodrow Wilson suffered a stroke that left him partially disabled for years. In neither case was the disability provision of the Constitution invoked.

AMENDMENT XXVI
Adopted by Congress: March 23, 1971
Ratified: July 1, 1971

Section 1
The right of citizens of the United States, who are eighteen years of age or older, to vote shall not be denied or abridged by the United States or by any State on account of age.

Section 2
The Congress shall have power to enforce this article by appropriate legislation.

★ The controversy over the Vietnam War gave a particular urgency to the question of whether Americans old enough at 18 to serve in the military should be denied the vote until they were 21. In the Voting Rights Act of 1970 Congress attempted to lower the voting age by statute for all elections, on the federal, state, and local levels. But the Supreme Court held that same year that Congress could establish the voting age only for federal elections, making this amendment necessary. After it was adopted by Congress, it took just a little over three months before it was ratified by the necessary number of states—the fastest ratification of any amendment.

AMENDMENT XXVII

Adopted by Congress: September, 1789
Ratified: May 7, 1992

No law, varying the compensation for the services of the Senators and Representatives, shall take effect, until an election of representatives shall have intervened.

★ It took this amendment over 200 years to find its way into the Constitution. It was first proposed by James Madison on June 8, 1789 when he submitted to Congress the amendments that became the Bill of Rights. Its intention was to prevent Congress from voting itself a pay raise by requiring that no increase could take effect until after the next Congress had been voted in. Transmitted to the states that September, it failed to be ratified by the necessary three quarters. There the matter stood for nearly two centuries, until 1982, when Gregory Watson, an undergraduate at the University of Texas, wrote a paper about it. Later he would become a legislative aide in Austin. Convinced that the idea deserved a place in the Constitution, he started a letter writing campaign to state legislatures. In 1939 the Supreme Court had ruled that any amendment could be ratified at any time after its transmission to the states, so long as no time-limit for that process had been set within the text. By the spring of 1992, 41 states had approved the amendment, making it part of the Constitution.

Relive History
At the National
Constitution Center

L OOKING TO LEARN MORE ABOUT THE DOCUMENT AT THE
heart of American life? The National Constitution Center is the
first and only nonprofit, nonpartisan institution devoted to the
U.S. Constitution. Located on Independence Mall in Philadelphia, the center offers a state-of-the-art museum experience, with hundreds of interactive exhibits, films and rare artifacts. Temporary feature
exhibitions have included *Discover the Real George Washington, Lincoln:
The Constitution and the Civil War,* and *Spies, Traitors and Saboteurs: Fear
and Freedom in America.* There's also a projected and live theatrical production called *Freedom Rising,* as well as Signers' Hall, where visitors can
sign the Constitution alongside 42 life-size, bronze statues of the Founding Fathers.

As a forum for constitutional dialogue, the center brings together leaders
of government, public policy, journalism, and scholarship for public discussions and debates. And it houses the Annenberg Center for Education and
Outreach, which offers learning resources both onsite and online.

Each year, the center also awards the Liberty Medal to men and
women who have worked to secure the blessings of liberty to people the
world over. The Medal's roster of recipients includes Nelson Mandela,
Sandra Day O'Connor, Kofi Annan, Shimon Peres, and Colin Powell.

*For more information about the Center and its programs, call 215-409-6700
or visit www.constitutioncenter.org.*

(AT TOP) THE NATIONAL
CONSTITUTION CENTER;
(ABOVE LEFT) A VISITOR
USES THE INTERACTIVE
AMERICAN NATIONAL TREE
TO LEARN ABOUT PEOPLE
WHO HAVE MADE AN
IMPACT ON THE CONSTI-
TUTION; (ABOVE RIGHT)
FIGURES IN SIGNERS'
HALL; (AT LEFT) GEORGE
H.W. BUSH AND BONO
AT THE CENTER